Marc

Adventures In Legal Land

Where black is white
and white is black
and other shocking discoveries
from America's courtrooms

Written by Marc Stevens

This book is registered with the Writers Guild of America December 2002.

ISBN #0-615-12299-X

Cover designs by Marc Stevens, artwork by Annette Smith of Mesa, Arizona.

1st printing December 2002, Mesa, Arizona by Marc Stevens.
2nd printing August 2003, by Marc Stevens
3rd printing May 2005, by Marc Stevens

This book was written, edited, formatted, designed, illustrated and produced in the *real* world-not in Legal Land.

This book is dedicated to my wonderful wife, without whom this would have never come about.

It is easy to believe that something must be true because everyone else believes it. But the truth often only comes to light by daring to question the unquestionable, by doubting notions which are so commonly believed that they are taken for granted.

Author Unknown

Contents

Acknowledgements

I first need to acknowledge my wife and the contributions she made to this book. In addition to being so creative, she kept me focused and from going into left field.

Annette Smith of Mesa, Arizona. Annette did the great artwork on the covers. She's an extraordinary artist and I highly recommend her. She can be reached by email at Adsmith1958@aol.com.

Moses was also a big help in getting this work finished; the many hours on the phone discussing the absurdities of "Legal Land," his edits, forward and contributions to the text. My long time friend Stan was an invaluable help with getting everything ready for printing.

And my children who never lacked a wise crack (*you're* writing a book?), but also had some good suggestions for this work – "D's" suggestion led to finding Annette. And *especially* when they *finally* went to sleep by 11:00 p.m. so I could work on this book.

I also want to thank and acknowledge my friends who I've helped over the years. They have contributed far more than just material for this book. I've left their names out only because these good people have had enough trouble from professional parasites.

And of course a special thanks to "Z" for being kind enough to be the model for the maniac on the front cover.

Foreword

If you want to experience truth, justice, freedom, *and* equality *within your lifetime* then *this* is *the* book for *you*. There is just *one* problem! Bureaucrats *everywhere* make the attainment of those ideals difficult or impossible based *solely* upon your *place* of birth ("your citizenship") and your geographic location ("your residence"). As a result, their *pretense* of good faith and fair dealing does *not* match your day-in and day-out reality. If, after reading this book, you come to the same conclusion, and you find that you actually *want* to *do something* about it, then you *are free* to do so.

There is, however, one important distinction between this book and other books that have come before it. *This book does not* tell you *what* to think. Instead, the author makes suggestions on *how* to think using a very simple approach that you may have once used as a child but you gradually *stopped* using (and eventually forgot) because you began to notice that it only got you in trouble whenever you tried to use it again. Well, here it is once again in order to help you *remember*, although, you *need* to realize that this skill was born *within* you and was always waiting to come out once again. Once you start to utilize this skill again you'll take your first steps into a world that you did not even know existed, and, it is at *that* point that you will finally be able to say, "now I've seen *everything*."

One warning before you begin reading this book, don't be fooled by its price; it is worth its weight in gold. This is because it says more, and with fewer words, than any such book ever to come before it. It is *even entertaining*. Rather than *boring* you to death with "legalese," argument, "legal" interpretation and the "law," or what you are being *told* is, or was, the "law." No, this book deals with *easily* discernable facts that a non-lawyer layman, with nothing more than the ability to read, can and will understand, and not mere "legal" opinions. That's right, *facts* that you can actually *rely* on because they will appear so obvious to you, once exposed to them, that you may feel you are *losing your mind.* If you disagree, however much you may *want* to disagree because the conclusions found herein are not "politically correct," you will find yourself *agreeing* whether you want to *or not* and whether you'll be able to admit this to yourself, and others, or not. *Facts* about the way things *really* are and the way that they *really* work that *you* can easily establish *for yourself, without* a lawyer, just by asking the questions found herein should you care to. And you *won't* have to become a self-appointed legal scholar either in order to do it.

My only regret is that I cannot claim responsibility for this book; *clear* and *consistent* in its message, *devastating* in its simplicity. Indeed, this is one of those rare literary works produced throughout history that has the potential to spark a revolution, not a violent one involving armies, but a peaceful one *within yourself.* Yes, here's to the final frontier of the human adventure and to those among you that will one day be known as the "Potentials," pioneers in that destiny, a *non-violent* world *that actually makes sense.* Oh, the *genius* of it! If I had *only* thought of it *first*! *Enjoy.*

Moses Antonio, November 2002

Preface

This isn't a book about "how to win" conflicts with bureaucrats or a "self-help" book. This book contains some of my experiences in various courts, especially tax and traffic related "proceedings." This is what I've learned about the true nature of these violent, humiliating, and ultimately self-defeating events.

"Winning" is a very misleading word though. In my experience, once you've had *any* communication with them then you've *already* lost. By bureaucrat I mean *any* "cop," "judge," "lawyer," "government" employee or any other "agent" of any pretended "state." A "bureaucrat" herein is any individual who does not deal with people on a mutual voluntary basis; what I call "*compulsory trade*." I say you've already lost because, at the very least, they've cost you your valuable and otherwise *productive* time, and I don't mean just the stop on the street either or the time you take to read their "friendly" mail. For example, if you get a traffic ticket and decide to just pay it, then the productive time you spent earning that money is lost when handed over to the bureaucrat. You didn't work for yourself or your family. No, *you worked for a bureaucrat* who did *nothing* productive to be entitled to your money. By productive, I mean creating value, value people are willing to freely exchange.

If you instead decide to have what politicians call a "trial," then *that* time spent is wasted. And if by some miracle, you somehow "win," traffic court is *not* where you will be "awarded" money for your time spent. This is true even if you "win" and prove there was no basis for the ticket in the first place. The only way you will ever "win" with bureaucrats is your being wiser for the experience and possibly learning one more way to keep communication with bureaucrats to an absolute minimum.

I "won" a traffic case in an Arizona "justice court" in December 1995. I "won" because the "cop" admitted he was not qualified to *write* traffic tickets. Despite driving out there (4 hours total) and my time at the so-called "trial," I was not given anything to compensate for my loss of productive time, except experience.

There are universal rules at work here. *With bureaucrats you always lose.* This is because, whenever you find yourself being forced to deal with them, *nothing* productive is being done.

**Bureaucrats don't create value,
they only take it.**

Bureaucrats feed off the productive. I keep this in mind if I ever get a ticket or any other communication from them. *Either way I am going to lose my valuable time, it's only a matter of degree.* Remember, that's how a bureaucrat lives: *off of your productive time.* As long as there are bureaucrats, your productive time may be forcibly or violently taken. Things will not change when the bureaucrats enjoy such mass support, whether actual or pretended.

I think of it as "damage control." Once a bureaucrat sets his guns on me then I am *going* to be damaged. I only need to decide what is the best way to keep the damage to a minimum.

> "No man's life, liberty, or property are safe while the legislature is in session." Mark Twain

This book is written about personal experiences, some seven years or so in the traffic, tax, and other courts from the standpoint of the victim. I have consulted with and helped people who had traffic tickets and other harassment from bureaucrats in Arizona, California, Washington, New York, Nevada, Colorado, Florida, Oregon, New Mexico, Ohio, Pennsylvania, Michigan, Missouri, Idaho, Utah, Oklahoma, Texas, Maine, Virginia, Indiana and North Carolina. During this time, I have noticed things are generally the same no matter where you are. There are some subtle differences here and there, but they are usually just in form, not in substance. While you may be *geographically* located in Washington, when in a "traffic court," or any American "court" for that matter, you enter what I call "Legal Land." This is the place where bureaucrats live. As the Cheshire Cat put it, in Lewis Carroll's "Alice's Adventures in Wonderland," "the only sense is *nonsense*."

The good news is, because of the way bureaucrats operate, and after spending some time with them, it's fairly easy to predict how they will react and what they will say in any given circumstance.

I wrote a script for a woman who had a case in the

Yuma, Arizona "justice court." Her husband went to court with her and called me afterwards amazed I predicted what the "judge" said almost verbatim. He asked how I was able to do that. I told him it was easy, all bureaucrats operate the same way. The only real differences are the individual reactions. As will be shown in this book, bureaucrats, if faced with certain questions, will always sacrifice one of two things and in doing so will show there is no "case." However, don't misunderstand, this does not mean a "case" will be thrown out.

To do this, it's important to know who and what you are dealing with. Understand as you are reading this, the *principles* are what are important here and not the particular examples I use in order to demonstrate a point. The fact I often refer to traffic "courts" does *not* mean the same thing does not apply to any type of "court."

Introduction

Going to court is usually a very intimidating, humiliating and sometimes *degrading* experience. Lawyers and other bureaucrats probably designed it that way. There is always a risk of going to jail for "contempt" if the "judge" gets ticked off or just doesn't like you. I have often wondered what it would be like if a "judge" came prancing out of his chambers and the whole gallery of people in the "courtroom" were also wearing black robes.

While most people look at traffic courts or *any* "court," as a "necessary evil," they might be surprised at the underlying *violent* nature of it all. I'm sure most people believe that if someone doesn't wear a seatbelt when driving a car, that they should get a ticket and pay a fine. But who thinks that same person should be handcuffed in front of their children and hauled off to jail, unless of course that person was *profiting* from such violent actions? What rational person thinks that same person should also lose his car because he didn't put a seatbelt on? Yet, this could happen *every* time a bureaucrat gives someone a ticket. Yes, bureaucrats believe they have a "right" to take your car if you are accused of something as petty as a non-violent traffic offense. Don't take my word for it, look up the so-called "forfeiture laws" in your area. In "Legal Land" it's perfectly O.K. to steal a car if you label such armed robbery a "forfeiture." In "Legal Land" a political label *magically* transforms robbery into something "honorable."

What I have found in my experience is that traffic courts are not a necessary evil. They are just evil. The people who do business as "traffic courts" do not tolerate challenges to their pretended authority very well. Most challenges, even if only in the form of harmless questions, result in a "judge" getting very upset and threatening physical violence i.e., "contempt."

When going to any court you enter what I call "Legal Land." "Legal Land" is very similar to Alice's Wonderland. It's where words and phrases mean whatever a "judge" or other lawyer thinks they should mean. This is a fantasy world where theft and violence are O.K. if you have a *badge* or a fancy political title. It's a magical world where facts are opinions and opinions are facts. "Legal Land" is where facts *spontaneously* become opinions and then turn back to facts. It's an enchanting place where slavery is freedom and submission to degrading and humiliating searches is a "patriotic duty." "Legal Land" is also where there are *millions* of ever-changing incomprehensible rules, but not one of them that's binding on the individuals who make up those rules and force them on others.

In "Legal Land," I've been threatened with "contempt" on a few occasions for merely asking a "judge" what *rules* applied to the "proceedings." How is that for anti-social behavior?

"Legal Land" is a place where you own property and at the same time you don't. It's where a person is competent, then incompetent, then back to competent again all within a few minutes. "Legal Land" is where an "error" is not an "error" if committed more than once. "Legal Land" is a place where reality may be disregarded as "legally defective" and a "nullity." It's a place where political allegiance is more important than facts. It's a world where being non-responsive is equated with "due process" good faith and fairness.

This book however, is not a "patriot" book with patriot type arguments nor is it a self-help book. I don't make any legal or political arguments that people are not required to have a "driver's license" because they are allegedly only for "commercial" uses of the roads, the so-called "16th amendment" was not "ratified" and similar types of arguments. This isn't an anti "government" or anti "state" book and I don't advocate violence in any form or under any political banner. I don't see politics as an excuse or justification for violence. I don't believe in a collective right to steal and murder nor do I believe armed robbery is O.K., even if you have a "majority vote" or a costume called a uniform on.

I believe parents are responsible for raising their own children, not mine. I have no "right" to have my neighbors pay for my children's education. I don't think my children have a "right" to an education at the expense of others, even if I or some faceless bureaucrats deem that education "necessary." If someone thinks his child is "entitled" to have their education paid for by another they should be willing to pick up a machine gun and walk door-to-door "collecting" it *themselves.*

This book contains my experiences with individuals who forced me to participate in their "trials" and what I have learned in the process. This is not written because I am allegedly bitter at having lost some traffic cases. If someone does consider me bitter, *so what*? Such uniformed *opinion* does not affect the truth. If you were mugged wouldn't you be bitter, does that magically relieve the mugger of responsibility? If people were not bitter lawyers would be out of a "profession" wouldn't they? I'll flip this argument around; is it a defense to a traffic ticket to claim the "cop" is just bitter?

Because of what I have learned, I personally have no political beliefs. I define politics as *organized violence and deception.* I believe forcing my opinions on others is wrong, whether directly or indirectly through what is called political voting. I believe that while I have the right to use my property as I see fit, I have no right to tell other people how to use their own property or interfere with their free use of it. I am not impressed by political pecking orders and I don't think it's "necessary" to initiate the use of violence. I also believe that no service, however valuable it may allegedly be, should be provided at the barrel of a gun. A service is proven valuable by the number of people willing to *voluntarily* pay for it.

Just because *you* drive a Dodge doesn't mean I have to.

In other words, just because you may feel the need to be dominated by another person such as a "governor," doesn't mean I want or need to also. If you need a "king" that's your "prerogative." However, your choice to shop at Sears doesn't obligate me to "contribute" a "fair share" of their operating expenses and if I don't, it doesn't mean I have to leave the geographic area I choose to live in i.e., "Sears: love it or leave it."

> "The thought of how far the human race would have advanced without government simply staggers the imagination." – Doug Casey, 1979.

Chapter One

Know who you're dealing with

One of my favorite lines from the movie *The Untouchables* is spoken by Sean Connery. There's an intruder in his house seeking to kill him and he says, "Just like a dago, to bring a knife to a gun fight." If I don't know who and what I'm dealing with, then I can't be very effective if I choose to "defend" against a bureaucratic attack. What is *critical* to understanding who and what I am dealing with is this:

> **Bureaucrats never ask permission to aggress against someone or their property.**

I know you may laugh at this, but this simple truth should not be overlooked because this is the basis of the most effective method of exposing their "proceedings" for what they really are.

If you think bureaucrats are a benevolent group of caring, peace loving individuals who respect the property rights of others, then ask a bureaucrat if they require your permission to "proceed" against you. They will tell you, in no uncertain terms they do not. In my experience, some bureaucrats will actually laugh if they think I am suggesting their "jobs" depend on *my* freely given consent. This however, is the reaction I hope to get. Let him pound his chest at what a *man* he is by not having to ask my permission to control my life and my property. **I never underestimate the importance of this issue because it's the only real issue**. I'm dealing with men and women who take control, also known as "jurisdiction," over people's lives and property without their consent *and are usually very proud of it.* In other words:

> **They acquire control over your life and property through violence and organized coercion.**

Why is this so important? Do you equate violence with good faith? I don't. Unlike bureaucrats in places like China, bureaucrats in the geographic area known as the "United States" put up a pretense of legitimacy. This pretense, or *public relations scheme,* conceals what is really going on: the taking of property and productive time through violence.

> "Political language...is designed to make lies sound truthful and murder respectable, and to give an appearance of solidity to pure wind."
> George Orwell.

Here political words conceal the true nature of what is going on such as "jurisdiction," "constitution," "nation," "state," "license," "court," "law," "statute" "arrest," "contempt" and so forth. This does not mean that I *return* that violence with more violence *because I don't.* I do the opposite.

Do you remember how the people of India, through peaceful non-cooperation, caused the "British" to show their true colors? The British slave mongers had a choice. Which one was more important to them: their pretense of legitimacy and civility, or their true violent criminal nature? Apparently, it was the massive lie their "government" put forth they were "civilized," that was more important. Gandhi and his followers were able to rid themselves of the British without resorting to violence. The English exposed themselves and then left. That is how I do things. I make the bureaucrat choose between the true violent nature of his "business" and his pretense of legitimacy knowing he's going to sacrifice one of them. I just hope it's the violence.

> **Political words and opinions are used so there is a perception that bureaucrats are a wonderful, benevolent group of men and women "protecting" people and their property.**

But it's just a pretense, fraud, hoax, swindle, charade etc.; without *violence*, bureaucrats could not function at all. If I took control over your life and property by force, I would be a criminal, and *prancing* around with a silly "crown" calling myself a "king" or a "sovereign" makes it no less a vicious act. And it still won't change if I get a few friends to prostrate themselves on the ground genuflecting and proclaiming me "king."

Change your perception for a moment. Look at the situation, such as a traffic stop, and imagine it without the legal *opinions* and costumes. *Just look at the actions and what is really happening.* This is similar to the story of Alice in Wonderland when Alice realized the so-called "queen" was just a playing card. Alice just stopped accepting the "mental conception" that a playing card was a "queen" and the "queen" lost her power over Alice. Another example is the story of the "emperor" without any "new" clothes. The real question here is, why would you call a naked man an "emperor" and not a naked imbecile?

A friend of mine was talking to someone on the phone

who stated the "Queen of England" was a so-called "sovereign." He asked what she was "sovereign" over and the guy told him the "people." So he asked, "What if everyone left England?"

As humans, we typically do three things with the messages we receive from our senses: 1) we delete, 2) add to, and, or 3) distort them. Because this is not a psychology book, I will keep it simple. Consider these deletions, distortions and additions to reality as opinions:

reality = facts
deletions, distortions, additions = opinions.

Everytime a bureaucrat spews forth an opinion he is deleting, distorting and, or adding to reality. This is very important.

A typical "traffic stop" involves a man dressed up like a "cop" committing numerous crimes against his victim. I mean crimes in the *lay* or *layman's* sense of the word, not in the so-called "legal" sense.

These are not considered to be crimes because, in "Legal Land," it's *not* false imprisonment, it's called an "investigative detention" or some equally inane political label. Nothing has changed except the label or opinion that's been added to it.

The political or statist "Legal Land" words cover up the real issue and *distort* reality. That reality is *someone is taking my property through physical violence, threats and organized coercion.* Don't *distort, add to* or *delete* anything from reality. Know who you are dealing with and don't bring a knife to a gunfight.

Chapter Two

Never assume anything

I don't accept *any* presumptions or opinions (delete, add to, or distort things). Instead, I *question everything*. (This tends to *really* irritate my wife). Whether I think I understand something or not, I *question it anyway*. I ask them to be responsive and explain it. I wouldn't just assume the guy who gave me a ticket is a "police officer" as if a person's *job* makes it O.K. to use physical violence and coercion against me. Just as important, I don't assume the "cop," the primary or sole witness, understands what is going on or what he is talking about.

I do not add opinions, I only look at the facts: *he's a man with a gun and a costume called a "uniform."* Not only that, he took control of my life and property without my freely given consent. I take this to mean he's a man with a gun who has no respect for human life; at least not while he is on the clock. In other words, *his job description is to be anti-social.*

When I assume or accept presumptions and opinions (delete, distort, add to reality), I relieve the bureaucrats of their *alleged* burden of proof and make the taking of my valuable time easier for them. If that is the case, then why put up any kind of "defense?"

Bureaucrats have to make what they do look legitimate, that is, give me so-called "due process of law," a fair trial *or heaven forbid*, administer *justice*. If the way they operate isn't seen as legitimate and fair, then people would not support them. At least not as many as do now. If people didn't support them, then they wouldn't pay "taxes." Without "taxes," there is no way to pay the men with machine guns to force compliance. Apathy has a strange way of doing that.

Let's face it, the only real difference between what the men and women doing business as the "IRS" do, and what a common thief does is the political opinion (label) attached i.e., one is "legal" and the other is not. Taking property by force is robbery and the victim usually doesn't care about opinions.

> **Whether something is "legal" or not is not a factual description of reality.**

I once asked a former "IRS" lawyer from Phoenix, named Eric, what the *factual* differences were between the act of stealing and the act of taxation. He initially *sneered* at me, "that's an easy question, one is legal and the other isn't." I told him that was *non-responsive;* I only wanted the facts. Just before slamming the phone down he spit out: "O.K., you're right, they're the same thing!" I guess it's tough realizing you spent eighteen years defending and profiting off of armed robbery.

This pretense of fairness, together with the fact that violence is the nature and basis of how bureaucrats operate, form the foundation for framing a very effective method of exposing bureaucrats for who and what they really are. They will actually expose *themselves.* I don't have to make any arguments or say that they have no case; *they will do that for me in their zeal to steal my property and productive time.*

> "Those who attack the rationale of the game, and not the players, are its most formidable adversaries." — James J. Martin, in the introduction to Lysander Spooner's *No Treason: The Constitution of No Authority.*

So again, the foundation for my questions are:

> **They operate by physical violence and coercion and they are supposed to administer justice, i.e., act in good faith and give me a fair trial.**

To rational people who respect human life these two points will *always* contradict. I ask questions to expose this contradiction. If you examine the opinions used to justify the violence, then you'll see contradiction after contradiction after contradiction.

Bureaucrats don't have to answer any of my questions either; being non-responsive also strips them of any pretense of good faith. According to their own rules, I am *supposed* to be informed of the nature and cause of the charges and proceedings and they *refuse* to answer any questions? Doesn't look fair to *me*.

Physical violence and justice are opposites here. In the real world, I exploit it as best I can. I have no pretenses; I know in "Legal Land" violence and justice are soul mates. In my experience bureaucrats have no problem using as much violence as is "necessary" to get compliance with their whims and opinions. It's just part of their job. No matter how much violence is used they blame it on their victim.

> "Yes, your husband's dead, but he had it coming. He should have had a seatbelt on and he should have answered the officer's questions *faster* than he did."

I think asking questions is more effective because the burden never shifts to me. Why should I have to prove anything? What if I'm accused of being the Easter Bunny or the Tooth Fairy? *Either way, they have no case.* This is true even if damage is caused. If you don't believe this, let me give you some examples although, don't misunderstand, this is not advocating causing damage. If I bust my next-door neighbor's window I am only responsible to him to replace his window, not some schmuck's down the street.

A woman telephoned me because she changed lanes without looking and damaged someone else's car. A "cop" then gave her a piece of paper known politically as a "ticket."

I asked her a few questions such as if she had insurance to cover the damage she caused. She told me she did and the insurance company was taking care of it. I then asked her if she believed she was obligated to the "cop" in any way. She initially believed she was. I asked her what *facts* she relied on to support her legal opinion. She was unable to answer. This is because there is no obligation. I told her I would ask the "cop" the same question. *When not permitted to delete, add to, or distort reality, bureaucratic attacks cannot be justified.*

Unless you've made an agreement by your *individual* freely given consent, then any so-called "obligation" is no obligation because it is based upon coercion. If this is not true, then consider the average thief on the street. If he sticks a gun in your face demanding money, are you *obligated* to give him your money? Even if you give him the money, are you obligated to keep giving him money months and years later if he returns? What if that same thief claims to be your "sovereign" and demands you genuflect after giving him your wallet?

Consider this, I walk up to you and say, "Oh yeah, by the way, Frank just agreed with me that you should be my slave, I mean *citizen*. We signed a contract, rather a *social compact*, now come with me and start paying your fair share by scrubbing my toilets." Would you "honor" such a "contract"? Would it be a contract? For any lawyers reading this:

> **Do you really think valid obligations are created by violence and organized coercion?**

I wouldn't think any rational person would think so because that would be the same as saying armed robbery is a legitimate business. However, in "Legal Land," armed robbery is legitimate *if* you carry a really cool looking metal badge and a high sounding political title. Lysander Spooner said it best:

> "If taxation without consent is *not* robbery, then any band of robbers have only to declare themselves a government, and all their robberies are legalized." Lysander Spooner, *Letter to Grover Cleveland*.

Criminals could also set up their own courts:

> "Banditti have not usually kept Supreme Courts of their own, to legalize either their robberies, or their promises to pay for past robberies, out of the proceeds of their future ones. Perhaps they may now take a lesson from our Supreme Court, and establish courts of their own, that will hereafter legalize all their contracts of this kind."
> Lysander Spooner, *Letter to Grover Cleveland.*

Having "courts," lawyers and opinions does nothing to make robbery any less of a crime. That is all political *slight of hand* to delete, add to, and or distort reality.

Lysander Spooner was a *lawyer* who competed with the post office bureaucrats who eventually used violence to shut him down. I highly recommend his writings, in particular his *No Treason: The Constitution of No Authority.* Most can be found on the internet.

My second example is that of robbery in California. I'll use car theft to illustrate. Without political opinions, theft is the taking of property by force without the owner's consent. Bureaucrats catch a man they believe took the property by force. This man is then put on "trial," he is "convicted" and put in a cage referred to politically as a "jail." The big question is: just *how* do the bureaucrats pay for all of it? This includes the "cops," "judges," "clerks," "detention officers," lawyers, "jurors," and the costs of running a cage ("jail") and feeding the hapless people stuck inside.

While the *political* answer is "taxation," the *layman's* answer is, "*they take property by force.*" In California, that would mean taking it from over thirty-five *million* people! Incidentally, "taxation" in the political sense, is also the taking of property by force. However, such theft is considered "legal." In other words, to punish and pay for *one* act of forcibly taking property (crime), bureaucrats commit the same act (crime) over thirty-five *million* times; and this does not include property forcibly taken from so-called "corporations."

You've heard the saying: "two wrongs do not make a right?" Well, I'd like to update that. In "Legal Land" it's:

> "Thirty-five million and *one* wrongs *do* make a right."

This is then hailed as "justice" and printed up in fancy "law" books. This does not mean I advocate the forcible taking of property, quite the contrary. I think robbery is *always* wrong whether one is wearing a *costume* or not. Bureaucrats wear uniforms. Non-bureaucratic robbers wear stockings on their heads.

> **Robbery is robbery whether done by an individual man or ostensibly by majority vote.**

A good analogy is this: you have two children and you don't want the older child hitting the younger child. The older child hits the younger child anyway. To punish the older child you *spank* him. This is even better if, while spanking him, you yell at the child, "haven't I told you not to *hit* your brother!?" However, to more correctly demonstrate how bureaucrats operate, imagine the same situation but instead of spanking the older child, you send him to his room and hit both the younger child and your *spouse*. You could then go door to door in your neighborhood *hitting everyone else*. If anyone complains, you just tell them it's the only way to punish your older child. Or, *it's the best system of justice in the world* and if they don't like it complain to your "congressman."

Bureaucrats never have a case despite all appearances to the contrary. If a man commits armed robbery and gives part of the money to some poor people, he is still an armed robber and his action is no less heinous. The act itself does not change if he frolics around like a nitwit calling himself a so-called "sovereign."

In "Legal Land" theft is O.K.; armed robbery is S.O.P. ("standard operating procedure"). This will be shown in greater depth later on. For now, I just want to point out the following. This shows theft is considered O.K. *with a cool looking badge and an anti-social attitude*:

> "A person commits theft **if, without lawful authority**, such person knowingly:
>
> 1. Controls property of another with the intent to deprive him of such property..." Arizona Revised Statutes (A.R.S.) § 13-1802 (emphasis mine).

Only in "Legal Land" can the exact same act be a crime and NOT be a crime. This is a classic example of distorting and adding to reality. Let's see what happens when we unravel this example of bureaucratic "reasoning" to see how far it extends. My edits and additions are ***bold italics***:

> A.R.S. § 13-1105. *First degree murder; classification*
>
> A. A person commits first degree murder if ***without lawful authority***:
>
> 1. Intending or knowing that the person's conduct will cause death, the person causes the death of another with premeditation.
>
> A.R.S. § 13-1508. *Burglary in the first degree; classification*
>
> A. A person commits burglary in the first degree if, ***without lawful authority***, such person or an

accomplice violates the provisions of either section 13-1506 or 13-1507 and knowingly possesses explosives, a deadly weapon or a dangerous instrument in the course of committing any theft or any felony.

A.R.S. § 13-1410. *Molestation of child; classification*

A. A person commits molestation of a child ***if, without lawful authority,*** by intentionally or knowingly engaging in or causing a person to engage in sexual contact, except sexual contact with the female breast, with a child under fifteen years of age.

B. Molestation of a child is a class 2 felony that is punishable pursuant to section 13-604.01.

A.R.S. § 13-1904. *Armed robbery; classification*

A. A person commits armed robbery if, ***without lawful authority,*** in the course of committing robbery as defined in section 13-1902, such person or an accomplice:

1. Is armed with a deadly weapon or a simulated deadly weapon; or

2. Uses or threatens to use a deadly weapon or dangerous instrument or a simulated deadly weapon.

B. Armed robbery is a class 2 felony.

A.R.S. § 13-2903. *Riot; classification*

A. A person commits riot if, ***without lawful***

> ***authority,*** with two or more other persons acting together, such person recklessly uses force or violence or threatens to use force or violence, if such threat is accompanied by immediate power of execution, which disturbs the public peace.
>
> B. Riot is a class 5 felony.
>
> And, *finally*:
>
> A.R.S. § 13-1402. *Indecent exposure; classifications*
>
> A. A person commits indecent exposure if, ***without lawful authority,*** he or she exposes his or her genitals or anus or she exposes the areola or nipple of her breast or breasts and another person is present, and the defendant is reckless about whether such other person, as a reasonable person, would be offended or alarmed by the act. (***This has special applicability to former "presidents"***).

While there may be a generous amount of *sarcasm* here to make a point, think about this: what is more damaging to people, theft or indecent exposure? Which one would you prefer to see "licensed?"

Asking questions can be a very effective way of getting to the truth; it's how we learn:

> "I keep six honest serving-men (they taught me all I know); their names are What and Why and When And How and Where and Who." Rudyard Kipling.

I think, if a person is afraid to ask a "cop" or a "judge" some questions then it may just be that part of them is already convinced they are not dealing with a benevolent individual. If someone has a problem *answering* a few simple questions then there are only one of two things going on: the individual has no answers or the individual is withholding the answer. In either case it is difficult, at best, to maintain a perception of legitimacy. This is the case if the bureaucrat gets angry with you for doing no more than asking a question. What kind of individual threatens a man with violence such as "contempt," for doing no more than that?

> "When tyrants cannot prevail by deceit, they burst into open rage." – Geneva Bible Note i, Exodus 1:22.

I helped a man in Washington with a criminal traffic case. The "cop" claimed this man was "within the state." When he asked the "cop" what facts he based this opinion on, the "judge" said the witness could not testify and, if any more questions like *that* were asked, he would have this man held in "contempt." This, of course, is "Legal Land" for having an armed man violently place him into a cage for the vicious crime of *asking a question.* It's similar to saying "collateral damage" for the cold-blooded murder of men and women and children known, politically, as "civilians." Can you imagine a "law" making it a "crime" to ask a bureaucrat a question?

Take the robe off the "judge" and imagine the same thing in a slightly different context. I'll use Sears as an example because it can be extremely difficult for people to stop deleting from, adding to, and or distorting reality. In other words, just changing the name from "City of Phoenix" to Sears can help to negate all of your previous conditioning, at least for the sake of this illustration.

You're at Sears and an employee ("cop") pulls a gun on you claiming you cannot leave because you owe Sears five hundred dollars. You say you don't understand why he has made this claim so he gets upset and calls other employees ("back-up") and his manager (the "judge"). The employee tells the manager you owe Sears $500.00 and you refuse to pay. You then ask the employee to tell you what facts led him to believe you owe $500.00. What did you allegedly purchase? The manager then yells that the employee cannot answer and if you ask any more questions like *that*, you are going to be held against your will ("jail").

If you look at what happens in a traffic case, if all you do is replace the name with Sears, then you may start to see the true nature of what is happening.

Here's another example. I helped someone in Sacramento. The "judge" was an older man named Joe. Joe refused to allow me to help this person at all. Joe threatened me with physical violence, "contempt," if I *spoke*, and mind you, this was not to Joe, but just quietly conferring with the man I was helping. How is that for anti-social behavior? Would you cage a human being for speaking?

After the "hearing," I politely told Joe, "I think your threats were unprofessional and unwarranted." Joe was not pleased and called a "deputy" to throw me out of "his" courtroom. Outside the courtroom, I spoke with the man I was helping and opposing counsel. This armed "deputy" approached me again and told me I had to leave the building "*now*." I said I was talking to someone and wasn't ready to leave. This armed man then threatened to "arrest" me if I did not leave.

I asked him why, and said, "Am I in contempt of the *building* now?" He made an approach and I told him to back off because I was leaving. As I was leaving I asked who the presiding "judge" was and where his courtroom was. It was a lawyer named Parks and he was across the street. I found out "judge" Parks was on the sixth floor and we got into the elevator. Before the door shut, two "cops" running full speed got into the elevator with us. We spoke to them and learned they were on a call up to the sixth floor. Along the way another "cop," who ran to elevator, got on. At the sixth floor, all three "cops" ran out and were joined by two more "cops." We walked out and followed them because we had learned, in the elevator, that they too were headed to "judge" Park's courtroom. As it turns out, they were called about me, though *they* were *still* unaware. After looking around for a few minutes totally confused because there was no "perp" around, the youngest "cop" eventually asked me if I was thrown out of the building across the street. I answered yes. He asked me who threw me out and I said, "Joe..." This "cop" looked very puzzled and asked who "Joe" was. I said, "He's the guy who wears a black robe and sits four feet off the floor." For some reason this really upset him and he snapped back, "You mean the judge!?" I replied that I don't look at Joe as a "judge," to me he's just "Joe." I was "escorted" out of the building and all I wanted was to speak to the presiding "judge" regarding my getting thrown out of the first building for no reason. However, just referring to the "judge" as "Joe" had a profound psychological effect on this "cop." And why is that? Because he was no longer following the "judge's" orders, just Joe's. *Not too easy to justify violence in the name of "Joe" is it?*

There are several other points of interest here: I was thrown out of the building across the street by Joe; despite five "cops" running full bore to "judge" Parks, no incident report was filed and, Joe was not brought up on charges by anyone for calling in a false report to the "police."

Say what you want about being thrown out of a courtroom, "let the baby have 'his' courtroom," but to also be thrown out of the building as well? And what about the building *across the street*? Exactly how far *outside* the courtroom does this superhuman power called "contempt" extend anyway? Maybe World War II could have been avoided by having a traffic court "judge" declare Hitler to be in "contempt."

Notice, I was in the elevator with the "cops" and they had no idea I was the object of their call. I must have been a *real subtle* threat that even the discerning eye of "professional law enforcement" could not pick up on it. And why no incident report? Probably because there was no incident, at least not caused by me. I spoke to the "captain" of those five courageous "cops" the next day and he asked why I didn't speak to him the previous day while in Sacramento. I told him, "Frankly, Sir, because here in Arizona *I'm out of range of your guns,* that's why."

Last, Joe was not brought up on any charges for calling in a false "police" report. If *I* had done that you can rest assured I would have been charged and convicted in short order. But why not Joe? My *lay* opinion, based on years of experience dealing with bureaucrats, is the "law" is not applicable to bureaucrats, while it is applicable to the *productive* of society they seek to rape, pillage and plunder.

I've also provided the "California Attorney General's Office" with documentary evidence of felonies committed by lawyers and have never gotten so much as a letter of *acknowledgement.* You would think that they would want to "arrest" me for filing a false report. In either case a felony was committed. So much for their zealous enforcement of the "law."

It is also interesting to note the "Judicial Conduct Commission" did absolutely nothing with my complaint about Joe.

Chapter Three

Never disagree with them

(Zen and the Art of Litigation)

I believe this is critical. I don't want these people ticked off at me any more than they already are. I could go to jail, or worse. While I have been threatened with "contempt" many times, I have not been thrown in "jail" for it. However, I do not think going into "court" and being argumentative is effective. If I disagree with a "judge" and tell him he's wrong, he's just going to sneer at me, "you can appeal." If I keep disagreeing with him, then he's probably going to start threatening me with physical violence and "contempt." The result is that I do not think disagreeing with a "judge" accomplishes anything positive. It only gets me labeled "argumentative" and I am viewed as an opponent.

Bureaucrats already view non-bureaucrats (productive people who want to be left alone) as the enemy so I don't want to help confirm this opinion. There is a very real "us and them" attitude with bureaucrats *especially* with "cops," and arguing with them doesn't do me any good and it might cause me harm. I know this from personal experience having known many people who are, or were "cops."

If a "judge" snaps he has "jurisdiction" over me, then I don't tell him he is wrong; as will be shown below, that's an opinion the "judge" can deny. It's far more effective to just ask him to explain *factually* where, when, why and how his so-called "jurisdiction" over me was *acquired*. I want to know where, when, why and how it happened so I can possibly *avoid* it. I put the burden where it belongs, on the unproductive individuals seeking to forcibly take my productive time. I call this **Zen and the Art of Litigation**; I am no longer the opponent, it's pitting the bureaucrat against himself. There is no fighting, arguing or other resistance, just asking for the facts and watching a bureaucrat's confidence collapse along with his pretended case. He may still be violent, but his confidence is declining steadily. It could probably be a mathematical formula, where a bureaucrat's confidence drops, his level of anger and violence rises.

A very effective question in this regard and one I've never had a *responsive* answer to is: "Except for physical violence, how was your alleged "jurisdiction" over me *acquired*?" This question may not be "denied" or rejected because *there is nothing to deny*. The "judge" has two choices here as with any question; he is either *responsive* or he isn't. If he's not, I don't really care because then he's showing his true colors. In a sense, without answering he *is* answering.

He could just keep refusing to be responsive, that's O.K. Every time he does this, his pretense of good faith and fairness wears a little thinner as does the patience of anyone taking his charade seriously. And that is the point here anyway. I cannot actually "win." I'm in damage control and I can only frame and ask questions designed to cause him to damage his pretense of good faith by not being responsive.

This is a "no win" situation for the "cop" and the "judge." The questions are framed to box them in and expose the fact there is no case against me; unless baseless legal opinions, political gibberish and fantasies constitute a case. Of course, despite no evidence, or even a hint of fairness, cases can be lost; after all, this is "Legal Land." This just proves justice and fairness is not the end goal of bureaucrats. No, the end goal is domination and taking property by force. The rule may be expressed in this manner:

> **Their purpose is to steal as much property as possible, using the least amount of violence.**

Some "judges" like to respond to such questions with claims the "Supreme Court" gives them the "authority," or "jurisdiction," over me. This usually sedates people and that is the end of the issue. However, this is still *non-responsive*, I have asked for the facts, not some obscure, collective opinion of a bunch of lawyers doing business as a "Supreme Court."

A "Supreme Court" opinion is just that, an *opinion*; the opinion of a lawyer and bureaucrat, it's not a statement of facts. Yes, it may contain a statement of facts, but that usually has nothing to do with me. A good example is *Marbury v. Madison* decided about 200 years ago. Factually this "case" has *nothing* to do with me or the absurd claims some "cop" may have made against me. It comes down to this:

> ***Who cares what a bunch of dead lawyers and bureaucrats think anyway?***

Do you really trust lawyers and bureaucrats? And if they are taken seriously, then why? Anyone familiar with bureaucrats knows it's not necessarily the opinions of dead lawyers that's the problem; it's usually the bureaucrats trying to ram those opinions down your throat at the barrel of a gun that's the problem.

Why would anyone care what a bunch of dead lawyers wrote 200 years ago if there wasn't any physical violence behind it today? After all, with enough physical violence behind it, *anybody* could force anyone to accept *anything* as the "law." If a gun is put to your head, then anything the individual with the gun says *is now* "the law."

The point here is that it's not so much the written word that's the "law" to be obeyed, it's the physical *violence* backing the bureaucrat's whims at the moment. One reason why people in Florida ignore the edicts, or pretended "law" of Fidel Castro is because *they are out of his range of his guns*. Another is probably *professional courtesy* on Castro's part. Professional courtesy may also help to explain why the California Franchise Tax Board only steals (*lay* sense) from people in California and not in Mexico.

Just by agreeing with bureaucrats and asking them to

provide the facts their opinions are based sets them up for a fall. By doing so they cannot convince any rational person I am being argumentative or putting forth “patently frivolous legal arguments long rejected by the courts.” They are either responsive or they aren’t; either way their “case” is breaking down fast.

> "Everything the state says is a lie, and everything it has it has stolen." Friedrich Wilhelm Nietzsche.

Chapter Four

Never give them something to deny

This is simple, if I give a "judge" something to deny, then he will. This lawyer wants my valuable time and it's very easy for him to deny absolutely anything and everything and then snarl at me, "you can appeal."

I realized this after a criminal traffic trial in a Mesa "justice" court (now *that's* an oxymoron) in 1995. I thought there was no way I could lose. I was charged with committing the heinous crime of "failure to produce ID." How the people of Arizona survived that "crime" spree is a testament to both the resilience of the people and the bravery of "their" finest public servants (there were no less than *five* at the "stop"). Who knows what would have happened had I just been allowed to go home that night?

I went in with a "Supreme Court" opinion called *Brown v. Texas*, 443 U.S. 47 (1979), that held you could not be arrested for not providing ID to a cop. How could I lose? I read the relevant part to the "judge" and he sneered down at me with contempt: "That's *your* interpretation." I was stunned, I had read from the opinion verbatim and he claimed it was only "my interpretation." Needless to say, I lost, and that is how things tend to go in "Legal Land."

The point is, arguments and opinions can be denied and now the bureaucrats can say they have been *responsive*, they just disagree with me. In "Legal Land," this is enough to satisfy so-called "due process" requirements, or what is more accurately termed the pretense of justice and fairness.

So, if I have to put forth an opinion or an argument, I just use one the "judge" and the "cop" have used. I send it right back at them as a *question*.

> **Feed their testimony back to them in question form and then *sit back* and watch it all *fall apart*.**

For example, I asked a clerk in an Arizona "city court" if a photo-radar ticket was a "civil" case. She said yes, that she had written the ticket. I then said, "is this in the nature of a contract dispute or a tort?" She started to stutter and stammer and finally spit out that she had "no idea." From her *own* mouth there was no case. At that point, all I had to do is ask her if there was a cause of action against the friend I was helping. How could she answer this question when she had "no idea" if the case was in the nature of a contract or a tort? Chances are she would answer yes. That's fine; I now have two conflicting opinions. Not only did I have two opinions that conflict, but, just as important, *neither one is mine*, so I am not the "opponent" any longer.

Pit the bureaucrat against himself.

It's now a question of which opinion will be rejected.

Bureaucrats, such as "judges," just *love* rejecting and denying *anything* a non-bureaucrat puts forth to defend themselves when attacked, whether in traffic court or with the "IRS." This is because there is a predetermined outcome. That being the case, I only give them their own opinions and fantasies to deny. It's like a dog chasing its own tail.

Q: How do you make a bureaucrat chase his own tail?
A: Agree with him.

Chapter Five

Take away the "judge's" discretion

One key to being effective is to take advantage of the so-called "rules" used to maintain the pretense of fairness. I want to do and say things that will put the "judge" in a position where he or she really has no choice. He has to either admit there is no case against me or he is going to make a huge mistake (error) that even the lawyers D/B/A an "appeals court" may not easily look past it.

One way to do this is to question the "cop" so his two lawyers, the "prosecutor" and "judge," have him declared incompetent, incapable, or unable to testify. This is *very* easy to do and I've done it every time. I never have to declare this, the "judge" and the "cop's" other lawyer do it for me. Actually the "judge" represents *everyone*, plaintiff, plaintiff's lawyer and the defendant. The specifics on how I've had every witness declared incompetent or unable to testify is described in later chapters.

When the "judge" does "rule" the "cop" may not testify, then I ask if his testimony, including the *ticket* the "cop" wrote and any police report relied on, should be stricken from the record to be consistent with the rules of evidence. In Arizona and federal rules of evidence, rule 602 requires witnesses to have personal knowledge of facts or they may not testify. This of course is a basic rule of fairness. I do not *tell* the "judge" to do anything, I only ask him if the testimony *should* be stricken in order to be consistent with the rules of evidence and fairness. The "judge" is really on the spot now. This is because under *their* so-called "adversary system" a "judge" allegedly has no discretion to declare a witness incompetent to testify and still rely on his testimony. Without too much legalese, it's unfair to rely on a witness who is not competent to testify or rely on a witness I cannot question.

Remember, it's not *my* opinion the witness could not

testify, it's an "order of the court," meaning it's the "judge's" opinion. That usually means that unlike *my* worthless, "legally defective" non-lawyer opinions, bureaucrats are *supposed* to respect and comply with them, after all, when an "honorable" lawyer gives an opinion *it's the "law."*

If the "judge" refuses to be consistent and accepts the testimony anyway, then I have two conflicting "orders of the court." One is wrong. Which is it going to be? I don't care which one as long as the reviewing lawyers are *responsive* and consistent.

If I still lose, then consider my appeal. There are no opinions of my own to bring forth for an appellate "judge" (lawyer) to deny as "frivolous." I just lay out the two conflicting opinions:

> The "judge" declared the witness incompetent to testify, and,
> That same "judge" relied on the testimony of that same incompetent witness.

This, in a sense, *sanitizes* the case on appeal. It's no longer a traffic case no one cares about. It's an issue of evidence and fairness. This is especially important in tax cases.

The lawyers reviewing the appeal, commonly called "appellate courts," hold the opinion that "great weight" should be given to a trial "judge's" determination of a witness's credibility; one example of this is found in *In re: Estate of Shumway*, 197 Ariz. 57. Well, the problem here is there is not one determination, but *two*, and they contradict each other.

I say, *go right ahead*, give "great weight" to the "judge's" determinations, only, give great weight to *both* of them. He said the witness could not testify, not me. If the reviewing lawyers fail to give "great weight" to *both decisions*, then there is a failure to review. This sets up a "no win" situation for the "judge;" in either case there is a denial of cross-examination. If he was wrong to decide the witness could not testify, then the refusal to permit me to question him (cross-examine) is fatal to the decision and "incurable." If he was correct, then relying on his testimony is fatal to the decision.

If I have to appeal, then the appellate lawyer, usually not the "prosecutor" from the traffic court, has to defend the "judge's" actions. If he is responsive he has to justify the "judge's" conflicting opinions. He has to justify why the witness could not testify and be cross-examined and why the "judge" relied on the testimony anyway. He has to argue that denial of cross-examination of the only witness is somehow not an "error."

This is why I have only had one appellate (traffic) brief filed against me or someone that I have helped in seven years. That brief was filed by a lawyer in Arizona and he misrepresented the truth. This lawyer just flat out lied claiming I never asked the "cop" about the facts. At least five witnesses would disagree with this lawyer. However, this is "Legal Land" where the facts are usually not relevant, only arbitrary political opinions backed by a gun.

In fact, in "Legal Land," the facts and the truth may even be seen as unimportant ***to a determination of the facts***. This is shown by many cases such as *U.S. v. Stepard*, 876 F.Supp. 214 (D. Ariz. 1992), where lawyers decided that *anything* offered by a certain non-lawyer was "legally defective" for no other reason than because he was not a member of a "bar association."

Lawyers routinely ignore anything brought forward by anyone who is not a member of their labor union, gang, clique or organization, usually known as a "state bar"

> "What Carroll purported to do for Paul in place of a lawyer was a nullity..." *People ex rel. Dept. of Public Works v. Malone*, 232 Cal.App.2d 531, 537.

When is a rock not a rock? When a *non-lawyer* makes the claim or presents the rock (facts) to a "judge." Or, it's called a "nullity." "Judges" say, just ignore it, their *political allegiance* is not the same as ours so let's just disregard everything these non-lawyers say or do on anyone else's behalf. In "Legal Land" it's not a rock unless a lawyer hands it to another lawyer pretending to be a "judge." I'll bet if a non-lawyer *hit* a "judge" in the forehead with a rock he'd *drop his legalese really fast.* He wouldn't consider the lumps on his head to be a "nullity." Just how many times does a non-lawyer have to hit a lawyer with a rock before he stops considering the rock "legally defective" or a "nullity?"

Let's use the same "reasoning" these lawyers use in another context. Let's say I cut a friend's hair and charge him ten dollars, but I don't have a so-called "license."

> "What Carroll purported to do for Paul in place of a *licensed barber* was a nullity ..."

> How about building a house?

> "What Carroll purported to do for Paul in place of a *licensed contractor* was a nullity ..."

What happens to the house in such a case? Does it *magically* disappear to be consistent with a lawyer's opinion? Would the hair suddenly *grow* back because a "judge" declared the haircut a "nullity?" Would it disappear if he was *reversed* by an appellate "judge?" My gosh, what would happen to a man who had heart surgery by a "doctor" whose "license fee" was, gasp...*lost in the mail*? If a pilot lets his "license" lapse, would a plane he was *allegedly* flying suddenly plummet to the earth killing everyone on board?

> **Is a dog without a "license" really a dog, or another nullity?**

If I drive without a "license" is that a "nullity?" If so,

then where is the crime? Can a "nullity" really be a crime? A "nullity" is defined by lawyers as: "Something without legal effect, being null." *Ballentine's Law Dictionary,* page 871, and "null" is defined as: "Nonexistent; void; of no legal effect." page 871 *supra.* If it's "nonexistent," then where is the alleged "crime?"

> "What Carroll purported to do for Paul in place of a *licensed driver* was a nullity ..."

What I see is that there are two kinds of truth or reality in "Legal Land," i.e., "legally defective" truth and "legal" truth. I call this ***"selective reality,"*** what lawyers call "legally defective" truth. It can then be cast aside and ignored, after all, what does truth have to do with "due process" and the finding of facts anyway?

Come to think of it, both the "state" and the "United States" were allegedly created by *millions* of non-lawyers. Would that make the "United States" a "nullity?"

> **Bureaucrats want reality to conform to their opinions instead of letting their opinions conform to reality like *normal* people.**

Chapter Six

Never argue the "merits"

I personally don't care what a "cop" has actually "charged" me with. I think the opinion, or "charge," as they call it in "Legal Land," is irrelevant. The real issue is his *method of operation* viz., physical violence and threats of physical violence. There is no way to use physical violence and still maintain a pretense of fairness or good faith. *One's gotta go.*

> **Those who attack the rationale of the game, and not the players, are its most formidable adversaries. –** James J. Martin

Arguing whether or not I have a "driver's license" or ID takes the attention away from the fact they are using physical violence and threats of physical violence. The whole situation is unfair, so why argue any alleged "merits?" *Who are they to force me to do or say anything*? That is the real issue.

A good analogy is a mobster "convincing" a businessman his business needs "protection." He'll make him an offer he can't refuse (maybe he'll threaten him with "contempt"). However, the "protection" is not where your focus should be, *it's the coercion,* the taking of money by force. The so-called "protection" is a superficial part of this violent scheme. It gives the *illusion* of a service and there is less attention given to the taking of one's property by force; it's called "sleight of hand."

It's not "the economy..." it's the coercion.

Can you imagine arguing with a mobster that he failed to "protect" you? The point is the actual charge is irrelevant because the nature and basis of the relationship is violence. As will be shown in later chapters, the central and most important issue here is: **what is the nature of the relationship**? If the relationship is based on violence then why bother trying to *reason* with them? Complaining and rambling on about "civil rights" usually doesn't stop car-jackers.

After all, don't bureaucrats or the "state" if you will, operate in the same manner as the mob? Let's say you want to start a business, such as a barbershop. You open your shop and start cutting hair on a voluntary basis. Several weeks go by and one day a bureaucrat strolls in and sees that instead of "licenses" hanging up on the wall, there are pictures of prominent mobsters. He tells you that you need a "license" to be a barber. You tell him you've been *profitably* cutting hair for weeks, with no complaints. Apparently you *can* be a barber without a "license." *He then makes you an offer you can't refuse*: "If you don't get the license the city will shut you down." This means armed men will stop you, violently, if necessary, from entering into mutual voluntary agreements with your customers to cut their hair at a mutually acceptable negotiated price. What a crime. Such a sadistic animal doesn't deserve a trial.

What is ironic, is at least the mob is ostensibly offering "protection," while the bureaucrat offers *nothing* in return. Yes, the public may think "licenses" are necessary for "protection," but as will be shown in the conclusion, there is no duty to protect anyone; it's an insolent lie. "Licenses" are about domination and money. You pay the"license czar" or you are violently shut down and, quite possibly, depending on the nature of the accusation, forcibly thrown into a cage. And why? Because you had the *audacity*, yes even the *temerity*, to provide a valuable service on a voluntary basis. Now that *certainly* warrants the use of violence.

Because the relationship is based on violence the actual "charge" is irrelevant. This however, does not imply that if somebody damages another person or their property they should not be held responsible.

> "Force cannot give right." Thomas Jefferson,
> *The Rights of British Americans.*

Chapter Seven

About the so-called "judge"

Going to court can be very intimidating. I think things are set up for that very purpose. After all, why else would a lawyer have to wear a black robe and sit four or more feet off the floor? If that's not enough to intimidate you, he also has an army of heavily armed men to carry out his every whim without exercising any personal discretion of their own. The "judge" is also free of all personal liability for his actions against you.

From personal experience, "cops" appear to worship "judges" and believe "judges" can do *whatever* they want while on the "bench." How do I know this? "Cops" have told me this themselves. "Cops" also believe they are somehow relieved from responsibility for their actions if done while on the clock or if "ordered" to do so by an "honorable" lawyer. That's the old "I was just following orders" excuse. While this was rightfully rejected at the Nuremberg trials of the Nazis for crimes against humanity, it is still a standard defense with bureaucrats here.

I called the "cops" on a "judge" while in the Peoria "justice court" back in 1998 for a breach of the peace. The "cops" showed up and asked me what was going on. I told them a man was threatening me with physical violence. I told them who it was and was told, "he's the judge, he can do whatever he wants, we can't touch him." I said really, what if he starts smoking crack up there on his bench? The "cop," a little ticked off at that remark, said, "Sir, he can't do that." Then I said, "Now that we determined he can't do whatever he wants, let's see about arresting him for a breach of the peace." The "cop" still refused to do anything. Why?

Because the "laws" don't apply to everyone, as bureaucrats would have us believe. The "time worn" line that "nobody is above the law" is political rhetoric or just plain old BS. In the real world, there are plenty of examples where bureaucrats do not follow their own so-called "laws." If you don't believe me ask a "cop" or "bailiff" who works in a "court" what you can do if a "judge" threatens you with violence. For anyone who thinks I am being too critical or I am "divorced from reality" or in an "alternate reality," turn it around and imagine that *I was the one doing the threatening*. And keep in mind that threatening violence is considered a "crime":

> "**13-1202. Threatening or intimidating; classification**
>
> A. A person commits threatening or intimidating if such person threatens or intimidates by word or conduct:
>
> 1. To cause physical injury to another person or serious damage to the property of another; or
>
> 2. To cause, or in reckless disregard to causing, serious public inconvenience including, but not limited to, evacuation of a building, place of assembly, or transportation facility; or
>
> 3. To cause physical injury to another person or damage to the property of another in order to promote, further or assist in the interests of or to cause, induce or solicit another person to participate in a criminal street gang, a criminal syndicate or a racketeering enterprise.
>
> B. Threatening or intimidating pursuant to subsection A, paragraph 1 or 2 is a class 1 misdemeanor. Threatening or intimidating pursuant to subsection A, paragraph 3 is a class 4 felony.

Notice this does not contain the phrase "if without

lawful authority."

Going to court is less intimidating if you remember the "judge," contrary to what "cops" may believe, is only a lawyer wearing a black robe and sitting four or more feet off the floor. Isn't it funny the "Wizard of Oz" was just a man behind a curtain, or robe if you will? *Interesting parallel don't you think*?

The "cop," on the other hand, is just a man with a gun who, more often than not, blindly follows orders for a paycheck. Everything beyond that is probably just going to be an opinion or fantasy, such as "jurisdiction." Remember, don't distort, delete or add to reality.

This is where they start to have a more difficult time. The bureaucrat is trying to maintain a pretense of fairness to conceal the violent nature of "his" proceedings. This is not an easy task for anyone. In my experience, the pretense is usually dropped very quickly and they resort to violence or threats of violence in most cases.

So-called "jurisdiction" is an issue where a bureaucrat will usually get upset when challenged. Although a "judge" will always *vehemently* maintain he has "jurisdiction" over me or some other non-bureaucrat in "his court," this "judge" will not be responsive to questions as to *how* this "jurisdiction" was *acquired*.

Getting upset and threatening violence (so-called "contempt") is part of the intimidation process (just like the "Wizard" did). I think the resulting fear is, of course, intended to keep people from questioning what is going on. If questioned, people might start to see the hoax being perpetrated on them. If so, they may begin to withdraw their support as a result. A "good citizen" is someone who doesn't question what his "public servants" are doing. A "good citizen" leaves everything to the alleged "authorities," he obediently listens when they scream, "Pay no attention to the man behind that curtain!"

Traffic cases are either "civil" or "criminal," although, in my "legally defective" non-lawyer's opinion, this is a superficial *political* distinction and nothing more. The only real difference is the:

> *amount* of your time they plan on stealing, and the *level of violence* they intend on using, or are prepared to use against me.

Bureaucrats tend to use more violence in so-called "criminal" traffic cases viz., they "arrest" you and hold you in a cage for a ransom, politically known as "bail." There is also a chance that, if found "guilty," they may want to cage you for a period of time.

The "benefit," if any, of having a so-called "criminal" case against you is there is more of a pretense of fairness provided in their pretended "rules." Examples are "probable cause" hearings, pre-trial discovery, juries and rules of evidence.

These alleged "rules" are not absolute. In my experience these "rules" mean *nothing* to lawyers and bureaucrats unless as a ruse to take your productive time. If these "rules" get in the way of a bureaucrat taking property, then guess what happens? The bureaucrat ignores the "rule" and moves on.

A great example of this is with what bureaucrats call "jurisdiction." The lawyers doing business as the "Supreme Court" have "ruled" many times the burden of proving jurisdiction is on the plaintiff:

> "**Federal courts are courts of limited jurisdiction**. They possess only that power authorized by Constitution and statute, see Willy v. Coastal Corp., 503 U.S. ___, ___ (1992) (slip op., at 4-5); Bender v. Williamsport Area School Dist., 475 U.S. 534, 541 (1986), **which is not to be expanded by judicial decree**, American Fire & Casualty Co. v. Finn, 341 U.S. 6 (1951). **It is to be presumed that a cause lies outside this limited jurisdiction**, Turner v. President of

> Bank of North-America, 4 Dall. 8, 11 (1799), **and the burden of establishing the contrary rests upon the party asserting jurisdiction**, McNutt v. General Motors Acceptance Corp., 298 U.S. 178, 182-183 (1936)." *Kokkonen v. Guardian Life Ins. Co.*, ___ U.S. ___ (1994), No. 93-263 (emphasis mine).

Thus, the entire burden of proof in so-called "criminal" cases is *supposed* to be on the plaintiff and that burden of proof is supposed to rise to the level of what lawyers call "beyond a reasonable doubt."

However, challenge so-called "jurisdiction" in a traffic court and the "judge," in every instance, will obediently do *the very opposite* of the alleged "Supreme Law of the Land" by assuming it for the pretended plaintiff or lawyer claiming to represent the plaintiff. I have never seen or heard of an occasion where a "judge" turned to the "cop" or "prosecutor" and said, "How about it, what facts do you rely on to prove jurisdiction?" Even in cases where I have "won" this has not happened.

Just change the *names* here from *State of Arizona v. Stevens* to *Tooth Fairy v. Stevens.* If I challenge "jurisdiction" in this case and the "judge" jumps in claiming he has "jurisdiction," it's clear the "judge" is *representing the Tooth Fairy.* It doesn't take a rocket scientist or a *juris doctor* to understand this is unfair but the rules don't apply to bureaucrats because we're now in "Legal Land."

And why should they follow their own rules? It's very shortsighted to think violent people will always follow the rules *if at all.* Violent people, *as a rule,* typically have no use for rules. Unlike *normal* people, they use violence to get their way. It's an example of bureaucratic nonsense such as "the rules of war." If these individuals followed rules there would be no wars.

I've had "judges" tell me straight out that the rules do not apply to them. That's right, "traffic judges" have told me the Arizona "Rules of Procedure in Civil Traffic Violation Cases" did not apply to an Arizona "civil traffic violation case." I've also asked, "then which rules *do* apply here," and have been threatened with "contempt." However, with the fear instilled by this "judge's" violent ranting and threats, how many of the people waiting behind me challenged him in any way?

> Bureaucrats use violence and threats of violence *because it works* in most cases. They get what they want from the productive without having to be productive.

If a case has been labeled "civil" the following questions have proven very effective. This is only with regards to exposing the truth -- separating fantasy from reality. Remember, there is no way to really "win" with bureaucrats. It's all about *damage control;* just limiting your exposure to them. Going in and disagreeing with them will make bureaucrats (or anyone for that matter) defensive and is counterproductive, in my *lay* opinion. They label me argumentative and use that as an excuse to run over me. *As if being argumentative somehow relieves bureaucrats of their professed duty to be fair.*

> "You're entitled to a fair trial as long as you keep your mouth shut. You have the right to an attorney, as long as you're not argumentative etc."

At the initial appearance, the "judge" may ask me what "plea" I would like to enter, "responsible" or "not responsible." This alone is degrading and certainly makes me appear to be the victim of this entire process. I like to say that I *intend* on "pleading" "responsible," however, I am not a lawyer so I don't understand the nature and basis of the charges and the proceedings. I then ask:

Is there evidence of a complaining party?

This is one of many "loaded questions" I ask, so I *always* expect an emotional response. If you are not yet convinced what is being done in a so-called "traffic" proceeding is "criminal," you may very soon. This is why it is very important to bring witnesses and a court reporter to court. People will not believe what happens in response to such a seemingly innocent question.

The "judge," however, may not fully understand what I am asking and may say, "the State of Arizona, *of course*." If so, I politely inform him, "that is *non-responsive*, my question only required a yes or no answer. I did not ask if there was a complaining party. I asked, is there *evidence* of a complaining party? Yes or no?"

I have never had a "judge" answer this question. No one I have worked with has had a "judge" answer responsively either. "Judges" react violently and threaten to forcibly put me in a cage. In the real world this *alone* is a denial of a fair trial and evidence this violent individual has no intention of being fair. If he answers this question by saying yes, I would then ask: "O.K., what is that evidence and who gave it to you?" Also, why are you relying on it without challenge?

Facts and opinions are two separate things and I'm supposed to be permitted to confront and question *all* witnesses against me. The most "evidence" that could be shown here is an opinion made with regards to other people who live in the same geographic area as me made by a "cop." I can guarantee that if I live in the same area, then they *don't* "represent" me as part of any so-called "state" or otherwise.

For those who may disagree, consider this: can someone really "represent" me if I don't freely consent that they should do so? *Represent me against my will*? That's insane, even if it's alleged to be for the "good of the whole." That would mean the "cop" *represents* me, or the very person he gives a "ticket" to. Does anyone think a slave monger "represents" the people he claims are his slaves? To "represent" me, or anyone for that matter, there must be something called a principal—agent relationship based upon mutual voluntary consent. This means I *direct* the agent and I may be held personally responsible for the agent's actions. Have you ever tried to hold a "congressman" responsible for not voting the way that you want him to? Then does he *really* "represent" you?

To represent means: "To stand in the place of." *Ballentine's Law Dictionary*, page 1095. Just who is this pretended "prosecutor," rather ***persecutor*** or "cop" standing "in the place of?" Certainly not *me*.

> The phrase "the state" is an **alter ego** or D/B/A for men and women who do business using physical violence in a given geographic territory.

I have found that the "cop," "lawyer," and "judge" use the same alter ego. Now, *how's that for fairness*? For those who may claim I am being "irrational" here, who do all three proudly claim to "represent?"

The "cops" and "judges" put forth the *opinion* the "cop" somehow "represents" the "people." However, in support of that allegation, they will put up about as much evidence viz., *tangible* facts, to support the opinion they "represent" the people *as I can* – none, absolutely ***nothing***.

It is physically and psychologically impossible to "stand in the place of" hundreds of people, let alone *millions*. How can someone stand in my place if they've *never had any contact with me*? I once asked a "prosecutor" in the Phoenix area to give me the names of the people from Page, Arizona he was allegedly "standing in the place of." You can guess his response. And yet, he had a burden of proof that is supposed to be "beyond a reasonable doubt." If anyone doubts this is an element of a so-called "crime," or "civil" cause of action, then consider who the *victim* or damaged party is supposed to be.

If anyone thinks it's easy, or even *possible* to "represent" a few hundred people, consider how many times the "honorable" lawyers D/B/A (doing business as) the "United States Supreme Court" have ever agreed on a *single* issue. There are only nine of them and they have rarely been unanimous in their agreement about *anything*. If nine people rarely agree on a single issue then what is the possibility that *millions* will ever agree about anything? Not likely. This is why there are so many major fast food chains; because *people don't agree* and are free to choose. Amazingly, all are in business at the same time, make a profit and don't put a gun in your face when they hand you your tacos or special sauce.

Another example which effectively demonstrates the idea that "prosecutors" represent everyone is a myth and hoax: It's clear that despite whatever opinion you and I may have held about O.J., there were plenty of "citizens" who did not want to see O.J. put on trial. I would venture to say there were tens of thousands if not hundreds of thousands of such people. Was Marcia Clark "standing in place of" those people? The answer is obviously no. She was not "representing" or speaking for them. When Marcia Clark claimed to be "representing the "state," it is clear "State of California" does not mean the whole body of people (politically) referred to as "citizens" and "residents" in California.

If you get a "traffic ticket," do you think the lawyer playing "prosecutor," or the "cop," for that matter, is "standing in the place of" you, your spouse and best friend? Not possible. In "Legal Land," it doesn't matter that a "prosecutor" is standing in the place of *no one*, except maybe the "cop" and the "judge," because all he has to do is to give his *opinion* and that is enough. In "Legal Land" the opinion of a bureaucrat is a substitute for facts. The irony is when I present facts they are labeled "time worn legal opinions."

In Arizona the "cop" signs the ticket as the complainant allegedly representing the people. However, this is only an opinion leading to the next question: "Isn't that just a opinion?" Depending on the answer, I could then ask: "Is there evidence, that is, facts, to prove this cop represents this group of people?"

This is also a yes or no answer. I could then follow-up with "what evidence is that, and who provided it?" if he answers yes. If no, then there is no evidence of a complaining party and no case.

Any citations to "law" or the "constitution" are non-responsive to the question because those are more political opinions. As subsequently shown herein, if the "judge" wants to rely on a "Supreme Court" opinion as *evidence* of "jurisdiction," that's O.K., as long as I can cross-examine those lawyers whose opinion he's relying on.

I would then ask him again and also tell him a responsive answer is desired. I may even politely ask the "judge" if he knows the difference between a fact and an opinion. I asked a guy named Paul from the Tempe, Arizona "IRS" office this question and he got very upset with me and suggested I leave the building. I only asked Paul the question because every time I asked for facts an opinion was based he would say, "Marc, the courts have ruled..."

This is not a superficial or "frivolous" issue either. If it were, then bureaucrats would not get so upset and law dictionaries would not define both words:

> "**fact.** A deed; an act; that which is real; that which is true, an actuality; that which took place, not that which might or might not have occurred [citation omitted]." *Ballentine's Law Dictionary*, page 449.
>
> "**opinion.** An inference or conclusion of fact which a person has drawn from facts which he has observed [citation omitted]." *Ballentine's Law Dictionary*, page 893.

Experience has shown this to be a very important issue. It's not unusual for lawyers, whether in suits, robes or otherwise, in order to justify the most egregious acts, to label facts as opinions and then call them "frivolous." This is also a favorite tactic of so-called "U.S. attorneys" in "tax" cases.

I have seen a statement such as "We received form letter [****] on May 24th, 2000..." described, by a lawyer, as being nothing more than a "frivolous and groundless legal argument." It's one thing for a lawyer to make such an absurd claim, but quite another when a "judge" accepts it.

I worked on a tax court case where the "IRS" lawyer filed a motion to dismiss and claimed the required lettered statement of facts was missing from the complaint. This was her grounds to have the complaint thrown out. We replied by pointing out the lettered statement of facts was "A through T" comprising pages 2-8. The "judge" agreed with his fellow lawyer by denying reality and threw the case out. The interesting thing is that, on appeal, the alleged missing lettered statement of facts was not mentioned at all by the IRS lawyers. Why didn't these lawyers defend their position on appeal? You have to also realize that this is not an isolated incident and if lawyers can get away with this in a "tax" case, then they can get away with it in rape and murder cases.

> DEFENDANT: "Your honor, I couldn't have shot president Kennedy, I was born in 1979."
>
> PROSECUTOR: "Your honor I object, that's a frivolous legal argument and should be stricken!"
>
> JUDGE: "I agree, and any more of those frivolous arguments and I'll hold you in contempt."

I'm still amazed at some of the opinions "state" lawyers throw out. It's as if they'll say *anything* they want to and feel they can get away with it regardless of how divorced from reality it may be. But, remember, this *is* "Legal Land" where deleting, distorting and adding to reality is S.O.P.

One recent "tax" case involved an appeal. The main issue was the denial of confrontation. The witnesses were not permitted to testify because they were determined to have lacked personal knowledge of the facts. Although the testimony (so-called "assessment") is "inadmissible" under the California evidence code at § 702 this "law" has never hindered a bureaucrat from accepting a fellow bureaucrat's testimony. Despite being an *incurable* error:

> "*** '[a] **denial of cross-examination** without waiver *** would be constitutional **error of the first magnitude** and **<u>no amount of showing of want of prejudice would cure it</u>**.' Brookhart v. Janis, 384 US 1, 3, 86 S.Ct 1245, 1246, 16 L.Ed.2d 314." Smith v. Illinois, 390 US 129, 131, 88 S.Ct. 748, 750, 19 L.Ed.2d 956, 959 (1968)." *State v. Hanley*, 108 Ariz. 144, 148, 493 P.2d 1201. (Emphasis added).

this group of lawyers, a.k.a. (also known as) an "appellate court," wrote:

> "***We presume*** there were other F.T.B. employees who provided, or could have provided, the requisite foundation for admission of the documents in question and could have shown how the proposed taxes were assessed by the F.T.B." (Emphasis mine).

Unbelievable, isn't it? As far as these lawyers are concerned, it's perfectly O.K. to deny cross-examination as long as they "presume" there were *more* witnesses you were *also* not permitted to cross-examine. Just exactly *who* are these alleged witnesses? Let's not leave out the fact the FTB previously *agreed* there were no other witnesses and the "court" was obligated to resolve all presumptions *against* the FTB. Yes, Mr. Simpson, you were not permitted to cross-examine Kato, but, that's O.K. because there were many *other* witnesses who testified that we never told you about that you could not cross-examine either. Now that's fair isn't it? Still want your *life* in the hands of "honorable" lawyers?

It's no surprise the three lawyers who decided this case did not want it published or even cited by their fellow lawyers, "honorable" or otherwise. To conform to reality, the above case should read:

> "*** '[a] denial of cross-examination without waiver *** would be constitutional error of the first magnitude and no amount of showing of want of prejudice would cure it, ***unless of course we presume there were other witnesses that were also not cross-examined***.'" (My edits in ***bold italics***).

You see? Sticking to the facts makes bureaucrats commit blatant errors like the ones I just cited. Again, this is because their M.O. is coercion and violence while maintaining a pretense of fairness. Can you imagine the riots that would have ensued had O.J. been convicted at his criminal trial and then the same appellate court (yes, the above quote is from a recent case, summer 2002, in California) were to *uphold* that conviction by stating:

> "***We presume*** there were *other* Los Angeles police officers who provided, or could have provided, the requisite testimony explaining why a vile of O.J.'s blood was taken to the scene of the crime and why there is blood unaccounted for."

Getting back to the above case, what if the "judge" tells me that he's not there to answer my questions? I remind him I would be *happy to pay the fine,* I just don't know or understand

----

is going on and ask, "is it fair for you to proceed when I don't know or understand what is going on and there is no evidence of a complaining party?"

If he tells me to get a "lawyer" to explain it to me then I would tell him, "I don't want a lawyer, I just want you to answer a few questions. Apparently, you think there is evidence here. Are you concealing that evidence from me?"

This brings up yet another issue about not being able to defend yourself competently. Lawyers hold the opinion that "only a fool has himself as a client" and that *all* non-lawyers are *incapable* of defending themselves. This opinion, from the lawyers D/B/A the "United States Supreme Court," was the basis for a movie starring Henry Fonda called Gideon's Trumpet:

> "**Even the intelligent and educated layman has small and sometimes no skill in the science of law**. If charged with a crime, **he is incapable**, generally, of determining for himself whether the indictment is good or bad. He is unfamiliar with the rules of evidence. Left without the aid of counsel he may be put on trial without a proper charge, and convicted upon incompetent evidence, or evidence irrelevant to the issue or otherwise inadmissible. **He lacks both the skill and knowledge to adequately prepare his defense, even though he have a perfect one**." *Gideon v. Wainwright*, 372 U.S. 335 (1963) (emphasis mine).

This is very important. Think about it for a moment. Wasn't I *forced* into this situation? Is it fair to knowingly force someone into a situation where they cannot competently defend themselves? No, it isn't, and it doesn't matter that I may be able to pay for a lawyer either. After all, why should I have to anyway? Yeah, some may say, "well, you shouldn't have broken the law" as if that opinion somehow *negates* the alleged requirement bureaucrats are *supposed* to be fair. Oh that's right, I forgot, a fair trial is only for people who haven't broken the "law." Don't delete, distort and or add to reality.

If the underlying proceeding is itself unfair, that is, based on violence, then how does hiring a lawyer make it any less unfair? It doesn't. It's still based on violence and still unfair.

I'll use an analogy to demonstrate this because I am sure lawyers or other bureaucrats reading this may accuse me of "mixing apples and oranges." Let's say a guy walks up and shoots me in the foot for no reason. No *rational* person would deny such an act is, at the very least, unfair. Now, is that act any less unfair because I may have insurance to cover my newly acquired, though unwanted, medical needs?

Is it fair for you, or a bunch of you pretending to be a "state," to bust my car window because my insurance covers such damage or because I can just buy another one? I could give analogy after analogy like this, but I've made my point. Just because someone may hire a lawyer does not make the situation any less unfair.

This is another example where I have them expose their contradictions. It's just not possible to give someone a *fair* trial when the trial itself is based on violence. After all, if there is a predetermined outcome, then it doesn't matter if you have a lawyer or not does it? This is why I always ask, "is it fair to force someone into a situation where they cannot possibly defend themselves?" Or,

Do you equate violence with good faith?

I would also suggest that without evidence of a complaining party there is no case. I may also remind this "judge" that if forced into a "trial" I will ask the witness i.e., the "cop," the very same questions. I tell him I am prepared to pay his "fine," if he will just be forthcoming and answer my questions.

He could also be honest and drop his pretense of fairness and *make me an offer I can't refuse* like other common criminals.

Another question I ask is in regards to the *nature* of the charge, in this case, that it is "civil" as opposed to "criminal." I ask the "judge," "is this civil case in the nature of a contract dispute or a tort?" This question really sets them up for a fall and always exposes the truth there is no case. If a "judge" *insists* there is a cause of action for me to "plead" to then he should be *willing* and able to answer this question. If he is so extraordinarily confident he has "lawful" "jurisdiction" over me, so much so he's willing to use violence against me, then he should answer this simple question; unless of course "honorable" is synonymous with non-responsive and violent.

I have never gotten an answer to this question and for good reason – ***there is no case***, they have no right to "charge" me, or you, with *anything*. This however, does not mean people should not be held accountable for their actions. Just as you are not personally accountable to me for not walking around with ID in your pocket, *I am not accountable to you or any of the bureaucrats pretending to "represent" you.*

A so-called "civil" cause of action can only fall into one of two categories: contract or tort. Yes, there may be more than one cause of action presented, but each "charge" must fall within one of these two categories. With bureaucrats they never do. So what is their defense to this if any? Can they just say, "a case brought by the 'state' does not have to fall within one of *those* two categories"? Yes, and doing so would be yet another admission their own rules don't apply to them. They only apply to you, their victim.

So here is the setup: A contract, of course, is an agreement consisting of several elements:

> "It is elementary that for an enforceable contract to exist there ***must be an offer***, an ***acceptance***, ***consideration***, and ***sufficient specifications of terms so that the obligations involved can be***

> ***ascertained***." *Savoca Masonry Co., Inc v. Homes & Son Const. Co., Inc.*, 112 Ariz. 392, 394, 542 P.2d 817 (1975). See also *Contempo Const. v. Mt. States T. & T. Co.*, 736 P.2d 13 (Ariz.App. 1987) (Emphasis mine).

The five or so lawyers doing business as the Arizona "Supreme Court," as well as other "courts," have long held that there must be a "meeting of the minds" for there to be a contract:

> "It is well-established that before a binding contract is formed, the parties ***must mutually consent to all material terms***. A distinct intent common to both parties must exist without doubt or difference, and until all understand alike there can be no assent. [Citation omitted]. If one party thinks he is buying one thing and the other party thinks he is selling another thing, ***no meeting of the minds occurs, and no contract is formed***. [Citation omitted] (contracts are founded on the agreements, not on the disagreements, of the parties. ***Where they misunderstand each other, there is no contract*** ... As the *Restatement* describes it, a contract is formed if there is "manifestation of mutual assent to the exchange and a consideration." *Restatement (Second) of Contracts* § 17 (1979)." *Hill-Shafer Partnership v. Chilson Family Trust*, 799 P.2d 810, 814, 815 (emphasis mine).
>
> And:
>
> "We [the lawyers of the Arizona Supreme Court] compiled basic concepts of contract law: "***The sine qua non of any contract is the exchange of***

> ***promises.*** Restatement (Second) of Contracts § 1 (1981). ***From this exchange flows the obligation of one party to another.*** 1 Williston on Contracts § 1 at 2 (1957). *Carrol v. Lee*, 148 Ariz. 10, 12-13 (emphasis mine).

Obligations (as even the "Supreme Courts" agree) are created by an "exchange of promises" not by the barrel of a gun or by some other weapon or form of coercion. "Give me your money or we'll put you in a cage, steal and then sell your house" is probably not the "exchange of promises" meant here. However, this is exactly the way the "IRS" and "U.S. attorneys" do business, although, they pretty it up with fluffy political language *as if they are fooling anyone* i.e., pay *your* taxes, file *your* tax return or we'll levy *your* property, prosecute you and then put you in jail.

So, if the "judge" claims it *is* a contract dispute, then, obviously, there must be a contract. But, in the lawyers' own opinion, to have a contract there must be evidence of an offer, a meeting of the minds, an acceptance, and consideration. That alone contradicts the underlying violence of the proceedings. I don't know about you, but I have never freely consented to anything demanded or otherwise required, by the men and women parading around, as a so-called "state." And it doesn't matter that I may live in the geographic area known as "Nevada." I see nothing in the above "Supreme Court" opinions indicating mere geographic location is an element of a contract. For example, I seriously doubt my neighbor is obligated to wash my car for no other reason than because he lives next to me.

> The sine qua non of any contract is *geographic location.*

While this example is admittedly asinine, it's how bureaucrats operate isn't it? The lawyers doing business as the "supreme court" tell us that *many* times such as in *Cohn v. Graves*, 300 US 308 at 312-313. Isn't that the basis of "America, love it or leave it?"

A good analogy I've used to demonstrate the nonsense contained in opinions such as *Graves,* is with Sears. There is a Sears in Houston, Texas. Sears provides a valuable service to its customers and also to that part of the community who never sets foot in their store. One way Sears does this is by providing jobs to people living in the general area. Those employees then spend part of their paychecks at other businesses in and around Houston. However, just because I may live in the same area does not mean I have an obligation to contribute to Sears' operating expenses. An obligation to pay a "fair share" is not *magically* created because there is a Sears operating down the street. What makes the men and women D/B/A Sears any different than the men and women D/B/A the so-called "state?"

Just because you drive a Dodge doesn't mean I have to. Just as important, just because I choose not to drive a Dodge (or pay a part of Sears' operating expenses) doesn't mean that I should have to move to another area (or *not* be permitted to shop or just browse in Sears), it just means I don't want to drive a Dodge, *that's all.* It should not be taken as an affront to the other people in the area.

Geographic location is not an element of a valid enforceable contract, not even in "Legal Land." In order for a valid contract dispute to exist there must be evidence of both a loss *and* a wrong:

> "**damnum et injuria.** Loss and wrong, the two elements which must exist in combination as essentials of a cause of action." *Ballentine's Law Dictionary*, page 304.
>
> "**damage without wrong.** Loss or harm resulting to a person which is not the result of the

> violation of a legal duty ... The practical sense of the expression is that there is no cause of action." *Ballentine's Law Dictionary*, page 304.

The "Supreme Courts" are pretty consistent here. For there to be a cause of action there must be both, 1) the breach of a duty and, 2) actual damage. See *Allen v. Wright*, 468 U.S. 737 (1984), quoted below.

No "cop" has ever accused me of breaching a contract or causing any actual or pretended damage. "Cops" blindly "follow orders" with no real understanding why they are doing what they are doing or what it all means. "Judges" appear to know this and that's why "cops" are never permitted to testify beyond a certain point. In other words, this helps to conceal what is really going on, not only from you, but from the "judge's" partner in crime, the loyal "cop" as well.

Despite this, I still ask my questions. If the question is answered (it never is), "Yes, there is a contract," then I would ask, "is there *evidence* of a contact?" And, of course, if this question is answered with a "yes," then I could ask, "what is that evidence, and where is it?" so that I may examine it.

The other side to this is a so-called "tort." A "tort" is defined by lawyers as:

> "**tort** ... A wrong independent of contract ... A breach of duty which the law, **as distinguished from a mere contract**, has imposed ... An injury or wrong committed either with or without force, to the person or property of another." *Ballentine's Law Dictionary*, page 1284 (emphasis mine).

Notice lawyers think the "law" is more important than a mutually voluntary agreement. To really grasp the significance of this, read ahead at what a "law" is.

A "tort" consists of two elements: the breach of a duty and damage. Here, the duty is not created by a contract or an agreement. It's allegedly created by the so-called "law."

There is no damage to anyone if I travel without identification, so *half* of a "cause of action" is missing right there. What about this alleged *duty* I am supposed to have breached; the pretended "duty...created by law?"

I'm only interested in facts, not opinions; facts speak for themselves so I leave the *legalese* or the *lawyerese* to the lawyers to make sense of. So, *factually*, what exactly is a so-called "law" and *where, when, why* and *how* did it create this alleged "duty" on me?

Have you ever examined *exactly* what a "law" is?

Before anyone can accurately claim or establish "beyond a reasonable doubt" a certain "law" created an obligation or *anything* for that matter, you need to know *what* a "law" is first, *then* you can examine exactly *where, when, why* and *how* an obligation or "duty" was allegedly created.

Think about this for a moment, if there was no "law" about having a so-called barber's "license," then there could be no cause of action for cutting hair without one. The "law" *itself* is being used against me and I'm supposed to be able to question *all* the evidence and testimony being used. The burden of proof includes proving the "law" created a duty "beyond a reasonable doubt" or, "by a preponderance of the evidence," in the case of a "civil" cause of action.

> "Words are, of course, the most powerful drug used by mankind." – Rudyard Kipling.

So, what *is* a "law" or a so-called "statute" anyway? *What* is it and *why* does it appear to have an almost *hypnotic* effect on most people? That hypnotic effect is probably due to the level of violence used to force compliance with it. But, exactly what *is* it, and *how* and *why* does it allegedly create any obligation whatsoever?

A "law" is an opinion backed by a gun.

That's it folks, that's all it is; the rest is just *political window dressing* as I will show. For example, a "statute" is just another fancy word for a "law." Even a "judge's" opinions are called the "law." Lawyers call this "decisional law." Lysander Spooner said it best:

> "What, then, is legislation? It is an assumption by one man, or body of men, of absolute, irresponsible dominion over all other men whom they can subject to their power. It is an assumption by one man, or body of men, of a right to subject all other men to their will and their service. It is an assumption by one man, or body of men, of a right to abolish outright all the natural rights, all the natural liberty of all other men; to make all other men their slaves; to arbitrarily dictate to all other men what they may, and may not do; what they may, and may not, have; what they may, and may not, be. It is, in short, the assumption of a right to banish the principle of human rights, the principle of justice itself, from off the earth, and set up their own personal will, pleasure, and interest in its place. All this, and nothing less, is involved in the very idea that there can be any such thing as legislation that is obligatory upon those upon whom it is imposed." Lysander Spooner's *Natural Law, or the Science of Justice: A Treatise on Natural Law, Natural Justice, Natural Rights, Natural Liberty, and Natural Society; Showing that*

All Legislation Whatsoever is an Absurdity, a Usurpation, and a Crime. Part First.

Lawyers, not me, define a "statute" as: "The written will of the legislative department ..." *Ballentine's Law Dictionary*, page 1212. The lawyers doing business as the "United States Supreme Court" hold the same belief, *see John P. King Mfg. Co. v Council of Augusta*, 277 U.S. 100 at page 102 to confirm. Simple observation shows us that, factually, a so-called "legislative department" is just men and women. If not, then what is a "legislative department," rocks, flowers, puppies, reptiles, raisins?

It follows that a so-called "law" is just the "written will" of men and women. We should not forget this "written will" differs from mine in that I don't force my "written will" on anyone under any pretense of "protection" and most assuredly not at the barrel of a gun. Does the "law" seem as sacred to you now? Don't confuse a political "law" with a natural law such as the law of gravity. The law of gravity is not the invention or whim of man; it's an *observation*. Just as important, when was the last time you were forced by another person to comply with the law of gravity? *And why is that*? Amazing, the earth rotates on it's axis everyday without a sacred "act of congress."

In my experience, no "judge" has admitted or *acknowledged* the so-called "law" is just the "written will" of some individuals *even* when he is made aware of it: "Pay no attention to the man behind the curtain!" That's why I request what is called "judicial notice." I request that the "judge" take "judicial notice" the "statute" I was charged with "breaking" is *factually* the "written will" of individual men and women. No "judge" has ever complied with this *despite* the fact taking "judicial notice" is "mandatory" under the rules of evidence. In Arizona, and in the federal courts, it's rule 201(d). In California, it is under § 451 of the evidence code. Try imagining *why* an alleged benevolent, "honorable" protector of the people would refuse in *every instance* to take notice of *what* the "law" really is. Why the refusal to comply with a *mandatory* function of his exalted "office?" Then consider this happens in every instance no matter what the geographic location. What are the odds? What are these "honorable" lawyers afraid of? It's called the "three monkey defense," *hear no evil, see no evil, speak no evil.* When confronted with *the truth*, "judges" are non-responsive. Their sacred "law" isn't so sacred when it's just the "written will" of some men and women.

I ask for "judicial notice" of what a pretended "law" is because the "cop" is *supposed* to prove, "beyond a reasonable doubt" this so-called "statute" created a "duty" on me. If the "judge" takes notice a "statute" is nothing but the will of a group of men and women, then the "cop" has to bring forth the facts he relied on to support his opinion their "will" created a "duty" on me to act, or not act, in a certain way. The "cop" is pretty ill-equipped to do this because his traditional accoutrements (gun, stick, badge, uniform, anti-social behavior etc.) don't help him any. In other words, swift and blinding violence is about as effective here as it is in solving geometry problems. Maybe "congress" can pass a "law" magically transforming everyone into a mathematician?

In fact, in every single instance where I have asked a "cop" what a so-called "statute" was, they were unable to answer; *they just don't know and lawyers don't think they need to know*. Yes, "cops" won't hesitate to *kill* you if they think you are a violator, but, while they are killing you they cannot tell you *what* you are allegedly violating. Has this created any "reasonable doubt" in your mind yet? This "cop" is certainly not in a position to testify he saw me violate a "statute" when he doesn't even know what it is.

> "Your Honor, I'm the one who discovered the theory of relativity."
>
> "*Really* officer Carrol, what does the "e" stand for?"

> "How should I know, that's irrelevant your honor."

> "I agree."

During one"trial" in Arizona I asked a "cop" if he knew what a "license" was. He admitted he didn't know. I suggested that since he didn't know what a "license" was that he was in no position to testify I was required to have one. What did the "judge" with the robe do? That's right, "judge" Donald bailed his buddy out; he asked, "Officer, do you know what a license looks like?" "Yes I do your Honor." The "judge's" response? "That's good enough for me." Not surprising that the "appellate court," yet another lawyer who is now a federal judge in the ninth circuit, "ruled" she saw "nothing wrong" with what her fellow politician did.

The "judge" is not supposed to have any discretion to permit such an individual to testify because § 602 of the Arizona evidence code states:

> "A witness may not testify to a matter unless evidence is introduced sufficient to support a finding that ***the witness has personal knowledge of the matter.***" (Emphasis mine).

If the "cop" doesn't know *what* a "statute" is, ***not what one says, but what it is,*** then he "has no personal knowledge of the matter" and "may not testify;" unless of course "personal knowledge" is now synonymous with gun, badge and a willingness to kill men, women and children for not "following orders." If this "cop" doesn't know what a so-called "statute" is, then it's *impossible* for him to prove "beyond a reasonable doubt" I allegedly violated one. This is much easier to understand if I don't use the word "law." Instead, I'll use "XYZ" so you are not hypnotized by the word "law."

COP: "Marc broke the XYZ your Honor."

MARC: "OK, if you say so; but *what is* XYZ?"

COP: "I don't know; *but you broke it all right.*"

Would you rely on this guy's testimony? Traffic court "judges" do everyday. It's no different if accused of breaking the "law" by a man who doesn't know what a "law" is.

I once worked on an "IRS" case with a lawyer. We initially lost the case and the "judge" used the "constitution" as grounds to throw the complaint out. We filed a motion to reconsider and requested the "judge" to take "judicial notice" the "constitution" was a "written instrument." This fact was supported by *observation* and by the lawyers doing business as the "Supreme Court:" "The Constitution is a written instrument." *State of South Carolina v. US*, 199 U.S. 437 (1905) *see* also *McIntyre v. Ohio Elections Comm'n*, ___ U.S. ___ (1995), No. 93-986, decided April 19, 1995.

This "judge" refused although it's *"mandatory"* under rule 201(d) of the federal rules of evidence. Without disputing the truth, she claimed the facts were "inappropriate." Susan's decision was based on the "constitution" but *what* the constitution *literally* is, was somehow "inappropriate." Yes, Virginia there is a Santa Claus. If you don't acknowledge *what* it is, you may as well as substitute XYZ for "law" or "constitution." *Tell me exactly what the "constitution" or "law" is without using the word "constitution" or "law" and you'll see what I mean.*

Nowhere in the federal rules of evidence can I find where a "judge" can refuse to take notice of facts because they feel it's "inappropriate." Relevant yes, "inappropriate," no. Couldn't the facts of a brutal rape and murder be considered "inappropriate" also?

You may be asking yourself *why* a "judge" would refuse to take "judicial notice" of what the "constitution" is factually, *especially* when her entire decision is based on it. After all, "judges" take a pretended oath to "preserve, protect and defend" the "constitution" and yet they run (sometimes literally) when asked to take notice of *what* it is. Why is that? I think it's because they know, or are realizing they cannot prove the "constitution" created any obligations on anyone. Can you explain how a two-hundred year old unsigned "written instrument" transfers property rights?

The same thing happens when I ask notice be taken the "law" is the "written will" of a group of individual men and women. Bureaucrats do not like talking about *how* and *why what* they call the "law" allegedly became obligatory (binding) or *how* and *why* it created some pretended "duty" they are accusing me of somehow "breaking." It's as if they know it's not binding on me, them, or anyone else, and they are afraid of "letting the cat out of the bag." Maybe "cops" would be less enthusiastic to kill in the "name of the law" if they knew it was just an opinion.

"I arrest you in the name of Ted Kennedy!"

I like to "cut to the chase." I may ask, "what facts are currently before you proving *when, where, why* and *how* the written will of individuals, ostensibly labeled "legislators," became obligatory on me?" They are the ones who are supposed to prove their case "beyond a reasonable doubt." How is that done without these facts? Can you just *assume* the "law" is binding? Yes, *bureaucrats do it everyday.* However, what is the point of a trial when facts are assumed? What about the part about "beyond a reasonable doubt?"

I did a pre-trial conference with a lawyer I used to work with. We were in San Jose meeting with two "IRS" lawyers. The lead lawyer snarled contemptuously at me, "What makes you think your clients aren't subject to federal law *Marc*?" I said, "What is federal law...?" She was a bit puzzled by this, thought for a moment and then said, "That's what congress says." I responded by saying, "O.K., isn't congress just a group of individual men and women?" She agreed it was. I then asked her, "What facts do you rely on that my client is subject to the will of these individual men and women?" She refused to answer and her younger co-worker arrogantly stated, "we don't have to prove anything like that and the court will let us."

I then said, "O.K. let me see if I have understand your pre-trial position correctly. You are saying, 'we're the IRS and we can do and say whatever the hell we want, not have to prove a damn thing, and the court will let us get away with it.' Is that right?" He refused to answer and they wound up refusing to return any of our discovery materials, including refusing to attend depositions. That, however, is typical when the opposition has no case. You see,

> bureaucrats believe they don't have to prove the "law" that they ram down people's throats is actually *binding on anyone in anyway.*

"Beyond a reasonable doubt?" Who are they *kidding*? Bureaucrats don't believe they have to prove their "law" is binding *at all*, they believe their *fantasy* is reality and if it's questioned, then the person who has the temerity to ask is labeled a wacko or being in an "alternate reality." And I agree in regards to the "alternate reality," my reality is based on tangible facts and a bureaucrat's reality ("Legal Land") is based on opinions heard from "honorable" lawyers and other bureaucrats. This is all just a "normal," everyday part of "Legal Land." Bureaucrats only need to hold an opinion (and a gun) and that's all. What is more, their *opinion* the "law" is binding and, or applicable is a *sacred cow* quite literally immune from challenge, the rules of evidence, confrontation and fairness be damned. And why is that? Yes, lawyers spew forth nonsense such as, "The courts have long held..." in defense of their "adversary system." Of course, who wouldn't defend their own business? However, legal opinions are not facts.

I once had a former "IRS" district counsel tell me over the telephone that if I were a lawyer, I would be "disbarred" for challenging a "revenue agent's" *opinion* the "law" was binding. "Disbarred" for challenging a witness's testimony? And why is *that* Mr. Former district counsel? You guessed it. Control. To keep the *truth* from getting out;

the truth being the "law" binds no one.

What would happen if just 100,000 victims of bureaucratic attacks challenged this legal opinion? Think about it. *It's only an opinion.* Confidence would collapse.

This is why a lawyer representing the "IRS" told me a "revenue agent's" legal opinions collectively known as a "NOTICE OF DEFICIENCY" were "irrelevant" to whether the "NOTICE" was correct (apparently the whole is NOT equal to the sum of its parts). In other words, his legal opinions, including the one the "law" created a so-called "tax liability," were "irrelevant" to whether the asserted "tax liability" was correct. That's the equivalent to "convicting" a man of rape on nothing more than:

> COP: "*He did it* your honor."
>
> HONORABLE LAWYER: "And how do you know this?"
>
> LAWYER: "Your honor I *object*! That's wholly irrelevant to whether this idiot is guilty or not. This man is a "cop" and his official opinion is more valuable than that of an accused rapist."

I was in an "informal conference" with individuals claiming to be a "Department of Revenue" in Phoenix. I handed the "revenue agent" her so-called "NOTICE OF PROPOSED ASSESSMENT" and asked her if everything on there was true and correct. The response? She and her comrades vehemently refused to answer the question. However, I think rational people would agree that she *did* answer the question by her actions. But why would people so extraordinarily confident in their so-called "assessment" refuse to answer this question?

Some may argue that whether the "law" is binding is somehow "irrelevant" to whether a "tax liability" is created; that a "revenue agent's" or "cop's" legal opinions should not be challenged as any other witness would be. I will briefly demonstrate why this is "irrational" and inconsistent with the very "system" facilitating the attack. *Real crimes do not depend on the existence of a "law" to prove they were committed.* I'll compare "tax evasion" with a *real crime*:

> "**Section 7201. Attempt to evade or defeat tax.** Any person who willfully attempts in any manner to evade or defeat ***any tax imposed by this title*** or the payment thereof shall, in addition to other penalties ***provided by law,*** be guilty of a felony and, upon conviction thereof, shall be fined not more than $100,000 ($500,000 in the case of a corporation), or imprisoned not more than 5 years, or both, together with the costs of prosecution." Title 26 United States Code (emphasis mine).

Notice this pretended crime depends *entirely* on the existence of some so-called "title" or "law." Without this so-called "law" there is no crime. The same is true of the affront to humanity called "failure to provide ID." Aren't "crimes" *supposed* to be proven "beyond a reasonable doubt?" Isn't the applicability of the "law" an essential element here? Can this legal opinion then be *assumed* by a *non-lawyer* (gasp!) and not be subjected to challenge? I guess "proven beyond a reasonable doubt" means spewing forth incomprehensible legal opinions. However, now compare 26 USC 7201 with a *real crime*:

"**13-1102. Negligent homicide; classification**
A. A person commits negligent homicide if with criminal negligence such person causes the death of another person.
B. Negligent homicide is a class 4 felony." Arizona Revised Statutes.

Proving a person caused the death of another person is certainly possible without this so-called "law" (person A pointed a gun at person B's head and fired...) Try making a case for "tax evasion" without a so-called "tax code." Let's see, ***person A earned $50,000 and put it in his pocket***. Yeah, *some crime*, shoot the bastard, he doesn't deserve a fair trial.

Just in case anyone thinks I am advocating or believe people should not be held accountable for their actions, consider all I am doing here is using the so-called "system" against *itself*. I'm pointing out the contradictions and inconsistencies. If some "revenue agent" forms an opinion, then that opinion is *supposed* to be subject to challenge and it doesn't matter what the subject matter of the opinion is. For goodness sakes, even "expert witnesses" are subject to "cross-examination." If you aren't supposed to challenge a "revenue agent's" legal opinions, then what is the point of having a "tax court?" If proving the "law" is binding is *not* relevant to proving "tax evasion" "beyond a reasonable doubt," then a bureaucrat could jerk some poor soul out of Fiji and convict them. In simpler terms, you could be convicted of not getting a dog license despite not having a dog:

"But your honor, I don't have a dog."

"That's *irrelevant*, the statute requires every person to get the license."

Then again, a dog without a "license" is a "nullity."

Wait a minute, I think they may have something here.

Do you realize men and women claiming to be an "IRS" and a so-called "Justice Department" bring *exactly* the same factual claim to your property as you do? Let me explain. You acquire 100,000 dollars. To prove you have a right to the money you put forth the following facts: you entered into a mutual voluntary agreement with another man to trade services. This agreement was carried out in New York. The "IRS" then claims 39,000 of it is theirs. What facts do they rely on to support this legal opinion? That's right, you acquired 100,000 dollars in New York; ***exactly the same set of facts to support your claim***. Everything beyond that is political mumbo-jumbo. And don't forget the New York "state" bureaucrats also lay claim.

Think about this: whether the "law" is binding or not is really a "jurisdiction" (control) issue so I like to ask,

> **"except for coercion, exactly *where, when, why* and *how* was your control over my life acquired?"**

There is *never* a responsive answer to this question. How does the "judge" maintain a pretense of fairness when he refuses to inform me of the nature and cause of the charges and proceedings? All I want to do is pay the fine and leave, *why doesn't he just let me*? There were times when there was a "release bond" I was going to assign over for the fine and they have refused to let me. They were *already* paid and yet they still refused to inform me of the nature and cause of the charges and proceedings. *What does that tell you*? Also consider I haven't disagreed or argued with him in any way. On the contrary, I've *agreed* with him, he has control and I want to pay him; I only want to know how jurisdiction was *acquired*. What's the problem?

Why would a "judge" refuse to answer a few questions and take the fine? I was once with a guy who put the checkbook right where the "judge" could see it, *it was right on the bench*, and he told the "judge" he was going to write a check for the fine because he didn't want a trial. This "judge" not only got extremely upset, he called in the "police" to have us "arrested." While our complaint about this was ignored, years later, the "Arizona Supreme Court" "censured" him for having an anger problem. Who would have thought?

A "judge" cannot be honest about what's going because he is the main player in this vicious scam. He has to put on the pretense; his dog and pony show called a "trial" is to provide the illusion of legitimacy. That is why he will not tell me what is really going on and just take his blood money; he cannot just be honest and say, "your money or your life" like other criminals. He probably knows the people waiting behind me would run out of there as fast as they could if he did.

What if the "judge" is non-responsive by citing a "Supreme Court" opinion as an answer to how "jurisdiction" was acquired? I would say, "*Really*? O.K., since you are relying on that opinion as if it's evidence, can I cross-examine the lawyers who wrote it?" I say this because the "judge" is relying on the legal opinions of his fellow "honorable" lawyers so I'm *supposed* to be entitled to cross-examine those lawyers too. I am unaware of exceptions for lawyers higher up on the political pecking order.

You see, *everything* being used against me is *supposed* to be subject to challenge. If the "judge" wants to order the lawyers doing business as the "Supreme Court" to appear as witnesses against me, *who am I to complain*? If he doesn't want to order them to be cross-examined, then he shouldn't be trying to substitute their opinions as "evidence" against me.

The rules of evidence are pretty clear and standard around the geographic area commonly referred to as the "United States." Two rules from Arizona and the federal rules are as follows:

> "A witness may not testify to a matter unless evidence is introduced sufficient to support a

> finding that the witness has personal knowledge of the matter." Arizona rule 602.
>
> "**Who May Impeach**. The credibility of a witness may be attacked by any party, including the party calling the witness." Federal rule 607.

In California, the equivalent is section 702 of the evidence code where it states "the testimony of a witness concerning a particular matter is inadmissible unless he has personal knowledge of the matter."

If the "judge" wants to be non-responsive and cite opinions and not facts, that's O.K., he's just digging a deeper hole for himself. Let him rely on opinions I can't challenge; doing so conflicts with his pretense of fairness. You see, this is not only unfair because the "judge" is now assuming the "prosecutor's" burden of proof, but he's also denying cross-examination and taking the testimony of "witnesses" who obviously lack personal knowledge. That's a pretty good list of "errors," wouldn't you agree? And that's all in the first two minutes.

I'm sure lawyers would protest claiming I may not cross-examine the lawyers D/B/A the "Supreme Court." *Go ahead and protest, argue, object and disagree*; rule 607 contains no exception for lawyers, even "honorable" ones in flowing black robes. I won't force a "judge" to be responsive. If he chooses to be non-responsive when I ask for facts and instead relies on opinions of his fellow lawyers, that's fine. I'm *supposed* to have the right to challenge all the "evidence" being used against me, including opinions, even those offered by so-called "expert witnesses" who are not even present or know they are being used as witnesses.

Lawyers can protest their own "rules" all they want; it only proves my point. It's the *inconsistency* that's important here, not whether or not I get to cross-examine a few lawyers. I don't want to cross-examine them anyway (have you ever tried to get a straight answer from a lawyer you're not paying?).

Besides, I have *productive* things to do. It just isn't fair for a "judge" to use opinions as "evidence" against me while, at the very same time, denying challenge. It only goes to show that:

> **There are no binding "rules" for bureaucrats because they just don't follow "rules."**
>
> **Just like peeling back the layers of an onion, the more you examine what these people say and do the more it falls apart under its own dead weight.**

Men with guns who have no respect for human life typically have no use for rules either. So, in regards to this, I just want to mention another political lie (I know that's *redundant*) before I move on. A well known opinion is the "constitution" allegedly established a "government of law, not of men" and a so-called "limited government," and "the rule of law." This is statist propaganda to the hilt and I'll show you why.

Regardless of what the "constitution" may say in any other clause, the only important one is the "necessary and proper" clause because *this* clause effectively negates the rest of that document. You want to know *why*? Because:

> "**Necessitas non habet legem ...** Necessity has no law..." *Ballentine's Law Dictionary*, page 837.

This definition (and the fancy Latin that lawyers will sometimes spew forth in order to confuse you even further) reminds me of many a traffic court "judge:"

> "**Necessitas vincit legem; legum vincula irredi-t**...Necessity supercedes law; ***it laughs at the fetters of the law.***" *Ballentine's Law Dictionary*, page 837 (emphasis added).

Yes, when confronted with rules, such as 602 and 605 of the evidence rules, "judges" *laugh* at the "law" and do whatever they want while *sneering* "you can appeal." Don't believe me? Try it and you'll see. Yes, these lawyers *laugh* at the very "law" they ram down our throats. Can you use "necessity" as a defense when charged with one of their pretended crimes? Still think they "represent" you?

As it turns out, the "Rule of Necessity" is a convenient political or statist way of saying bureaucrats can do whatever they want and the alleged "law," such as the "fifth amendment," is just not applicable.

A great example is in the "Arizona Rules of the Supreme Court." The so-called "*Supreme* Law of the Land," is that, if forced into "court," you are supposed to get a fair and impartial trial or your "life, liberty and property" are not supposed to be taken away from you. This is commonly known as "due process" (fifth amendment) or "having your day in court." This, however, is just not consistent with the facts. The term "due process," as it turns out, is very, very misleading.

If you look at the Arizona Rules of the Supreme Court, Rule 81, Code of Judicial Conduct (the "judge's" ethics rules - I *know*, that's an *oxymoron*), the commentary for Canon 3E(1), says:

> "By decisional law, the rule of necessity may override the rule of disqualification."

What this is actually means, when you strip away the lawyerese, is a "judge's" *opinion* is more important than his following the rules and giving you a fair trial, such as, recusing himself as your "judge" whenever he is asked to rule on any cause about which his impartiality might reasonably be questioned. To "recuse" means to "disqualify" himself, i.e., to step down from "the bench," that seat that he sits on behind a big wooden table four feet off the floor, so that another "judge" can replace him. In essence, it means:

By decisional law, the Rule of Necessity may override the Rule of Law.

If you cannot receive a fair trial, then they are not supposed to put you on trial at all or take your "life, liberty or property" away from you. However, lawyers and bureaucrats are not in the fairness business; that's why they completely disregard the so-called "law" whenever they feel like it by using what they call "the Rule of Necessity," *their* idea of necessity.

Whether you believe it or not will not change the reality there is no such thing as a "government of laws, not men." This is because the "law" *itself* is nothing more than an *opinion* "by one man, or a body of men," as Spooner put it, *backed by a gun,* and this includes so-called "decisional law," as lawyers call it.

A "government" is a group of men and women doing business using physical violence under the political banner of "necessity."

Their opinions are just political window dressing to conceal that violence. Go ahead. Conduct your own law library or internet search of "Supreme Court" opinions using the key word "necessity" and you will find the most egregious acts of violence that have all been justified by what *they* say was necessary.

COP "We had to kill him your Honor."

JUDGE "And why is that officer Mitchell?"

COP "It was necessary to get his car away from him."

JUDGE "Was he engaged in, or wanted for a

crime?

COP "No, but I hardly think that's relevant your honor."

JUDGE "Neither do I.

The fact that the "laws" and the rules of court do not apply to bureaucrats is shown everyday by the "judges" themselves if the right questions are asked in traffic court. Sometimes, you can see this for yourself even if you don't ask the right questions, just by having a basic understanding of what is right and fair. The issue of how the "judge" acquired "jurisdiction" (control) is just one; but it's very important, maybe even the most important. "Jurisdiction" is supposed to be an element of a so-called "crime" and a "cause of action." The burden of proof is *supposed* to be on the party asserting it and, in a criminal case, the burden is "beyond a reasonable doubt," while, in a "civil" case, it is *supposed* to be by a "preponderance of the evidence." *Supposed* to be. Remember, this is "Legal Land" where *nothing* is what it's supposed to be.

Well, it's bad enough if the "judge" assumes "jurisdiction" on behalf of the alleged complaining party, but it's an insult added to injury to also use an opinion against me I cannot challenge. I would therefore ask, "is the use of opinions I cannot challenge *factually* consistent with the confrontation clauses?" Using so-called "evidence" not subject to challenge is not a trial in any sense of the word.

For the lawyers out there, do not mix apples and oranges here or accuse me of doing the same. This is not to say an issue of so-called "law" may not be settled by citing an opinion of the "Supreme Court." On the contrary, this is an issue of evidence and facts, not of "law." It's also an issue of being responsive to a simple question. I should not be given an opinion when I ask for the facts.

Some may ignore that I asked for the *facts* and say it's

"well-settled law" that the "judge" has jurisdiction. It is also "well-settled law" that you're supposed to wear a seatbelt, so why have a trial at all when the charge is failure to wear a seatbelt? Come to think of it, **if I have to accept opinions without challenge then what is the point of having a trial under any circumstances**? If it's so "well-settled," then why not repeal "civil" rules such as 12(b)(6), one of the motion to dismiss rules? If it's such "well-settled law", then why do "U.S. Attorneys" *always* file motions to dismiss whenever someone sues the "IRS?"

The "judge" is *supposed* to be impartial and independent; not in *my* opinion, but in *their* opinion. This so-called independence would be subverted if he is assuming "jurisdiction" for a party. This will be discussed in greater detail below.

As stated earlier, a cause of action is supposed to require the breach of a duty resulting in damage. So, I may ask, "am I being accused of breaching some duty?" If this is answered, then the answer would most likely be "yes." I would then ask, "where, when, why and how was this alleged duty created?" Keep in mind this *presupposes* the "judge" has answered whether or not this "civil" case was a contract dispute or a tort. Chances are this question will not be answered. Most questions are not answered. Maybe "honorable" lawyers do not feel the need to condescend to my non-lawyer level to answer a question.

I would also ask: "Was this alleged duty created by coercion?" If that alleged duty was created by coercion, then why not also impose the "duty" to pay the fine by coercion and skip the pretense? Why not be consistent?

As previously stated, bureaucrats have most people blindly accepting their pretended "laws" so they don't have to worry about non-compliance. However, "in a democracy based on the rule of law and not of men," and other such "legalistic gibberish," the pretense of a fair trial must be maintained in order to keep those very same people fast asleep regarding the true nature of their so-called "system" so they will continue to go right on blindly obeying and paying.

After all, if a "duty" can be created by coercion, then how can the crime called "armed robbery" even exist? For example, you walk into a bank with a machine gun, you fire off a few rounds and inform every employee in the bank that they will die if you don't get all of the money stored away inside of their bank. If "legal duties" are created by coercion, then the people in that bank would have a "legal duty" to comply, now wouldn't they? If it is, then *where's the crime*? In fact, what is really crazy here is if the bank's employees *refuse to comply*, then *they've* committed a crime and not the guy with the machine gun. In "Legal Land" such heinous crime by the bank employees is called "tax evasion." In "Legal Land" violence is "honorable" and not complying with that violence is the crime.

The really uncomfortable part for a "judge" is in regards to the second half of a cause of action i.e., the damage. How can there be any "damage" if I don't have an ID card in my pocket? The only "damage" may be to the *ego* of the man dressed in a costume, with a gun and a healthy appetite for violence and domination because I didn't obey his legal "order."

What they are *really* accusing me of is *disobedience* to their pretended "authority," not of breaching any duty or causing any damage. "Traffic court" is a matter of obedience, domination and money, not a matter of safety, fairness and justice. They're determined to make sure that I obey the next time around. This is proven by looking at their own so-called "law." I can always rely on contradictions when dealing with bureaucrats. A great example in Arizona is found within their so-called "constitution"

> "Governments derive their just powers from the consent of the governed, and are established to protect and maintain individual rights."—Arizona constitution article II § 2.

If you think about it, bureaucrats *claim* to protect *everyone's* rights, yet, ***who's*** rights are they allegedly "protecting" if I am charged with not having an ID card in my pocket? In other words, *where is the "damage" if I travel without identification*? What about a "license plate" for that matter?

I have asked for the names of the alleged victims whose rights the fearless "prosecutor" is valiantly "protecting" and have never gotten an answer. Why is that? However, one persecutor in Arizona actually claimed he was "representing" *me*. Wow, I'm both the plaintiff *and* the defendant. Before anyone laughs, consider this opinion is not "legally defective," it was a lawyer's, a proud member of the "Arizona Bar Association," the only people permitted to give legal opinions in "Legal Land." *Now you can laugh*. If he was really "representing" me, then I would have been *complaining against myself*; I could have told him to withdraw the complaint. He was claiming to be "stand[ing] in the place of" me. But I think everyone is aware he did not "represent" me. If he did, then notwithstanding the complete lack of supporting evidence, there was a serious conflict of interest, in my *lay* opinion.

I hardly think that any lawyer, or "cop," for that matter, could produce any evidence that I, being in Phoenix, have obligations to people in Parker, Arizona, hundreds of miles away. To date, all have refused to even try. No, instead, they leave that "burden" for their exalted partner the "judge" to decide. All that means is that the "judge" bails them out because the "judge" can call his little army of non-discretion exercising henchmen ("bailiff," "cop," "deputy" etc.,) to throw me in a cage for humans with a so-called "command," "mandate," "decree" or "order."

It's even more difficult, if not impossible, for these bureaucrats to provide the actual "rights" they are courageously "protecting" or "redressing" in a "traffic" case. I'll elaborate. Bureaucrats *allege* we have a right to "life, liberty and property." In a case of car theft, the victim's right to property was violated. In a kidnapping case, the victim's right to liberty is violated and, in a murder case, the victim's right to life is violated. There it's clear which rights the "prosecutor" is allegedly "protecting" or "redressing." But what if I forget to leave the house with ID? If I live in Phoenix, Arizona, and leave my home without ID, how are the people at the Grand Canyon injured? *Which* rights of theirs have I allegedly violated and *how*? Was it their right to life, liberty or property? *Oh no*, all three? If you laugh, then keep in mind, this is supposed to be proven "beyond a reasonable doubt."

I've asked "cops" this question and the best they can do is say I "failed to produce ID." It's a stupid "time worn" mantra; they have no responsive answers *because there are none*. It's a fantasy to think people are damaged if I don't have ID on me. Why not accuse me of not dressing like the Tooth Fairy? That causes the same amount of damage to other people as not having a picture ID in my pocket.

At what point does this senseless violation of rights occur? What kind of person is so cold-blooded and insensitive to the rights of others they actually leave their house without an ID card? Let's take this one step at a time and see if we can pinpoint exactly when the "rights" are violated. 1) I decide I want to leave my home in Phoenix and get some raisins down the street. I have some cash in my pocket so, 2) I don't take ID with me. 3) I get into my car and travel down the street. 4) A valiant public servant, a "cop," ever vigilant to protect the people, *senses* I don't have ID. 5) Knowing there is criminal activity brewing, he turns on his emergency lights and 6) I stop my car. 7) Our conquering "hero" the "cop," bravely approaches the vehicle and with great confidence, *throwing caution to the wind*, 8) asks to see my ID. 9) I tell this courageous, selfless man, "I have no ID." 10) Our "cop" informs me that I am now "under arrest" and, 11) far greater tragedy to the people of Arizona has been narrowly averted by this altruistic "servant" of the people. Who knows what might have been the extent of the damage had I been permitted to continue traveling down the street? I could have bought some raisins (or other dry fruit) without ID! Oh, "the horror...the horror."

And, mind you, bureaucrats do believe not having ID is a *crime* warranting jail time. One lawyer from the Phoenix area wanted a "judge" to put me in jail for six months not because I didn't have ID, but because my ID did not have a picture on it:

> "**A.R.S. 28-1595. <u>Failure to stop or provide driver license or evidence of identity; violation; classification</u>**
>
> A. The operator of a motor vehicle who knowingly fails or refuses to bring the operator's motor vehicle to a stop after being given a visual or audible signal or instruction by a peace officer or duly authorized agent of a traffic enforcement agency is guilty of a class 2 misdemeanor.
>
> B. After stopping as required by subsection A of this section, the operator of a motor vehicle who fails or refuses to exhibit the operator's driver license as required by section 28-3169 or ***a driver who is not licensed and who fails or refuses to provide evidence of the driver's identity on request is guilty of a class 2 misdemeanor***. The evidence of identity that is presented shall contain all of the following information ..." (Emphasis mine).

Just how many tragedies has this so-called "statute" prevented? What on earth did people do in the days *prior* to picture ID's? No wonder they're called the "Dark Ages," *there was no flash photography*.

My question is this: at what point did this nefarious crime begin? If you laugh at this suggestion consider this so-called "crime" is supposed to be proven "beyond a reasonable doubt." Was it at step #1, when I was *thinking* of going out for raisins or when I actually decided to go out without ID? If my wife knew I was going out without ID would she be guilty of aiding and abetting? What if *she* suggested I go out without my ID, would she be guilty of *conspiracy* to fail to produce ID? Maybe she should have performed a "citizen's arrest" and prevented me from leaving the house? What if I thought about going out without ID and the phone rang and I didn't go out, would that be *attempted* failure to provide ID?

At which point did the people of Heber, Arizona, start having their rights violated and *which* ones? Was it the "right" to go to sleep at night knowing some lunatic was not out traveling without a picture ID in his pocket? Were the people of Jerome, Arizona, damaged at the same time as the people at the Grand Canyon? Are non-citizens and non-residents also damaged, or just citizens? What about people just visiting or citizens visiting the other side of North America, is it a *vicarious* injury? If it damages people 200 miles away, then why aren't people damaged in California and Mexico? Or are they damaged as well and "cops" just don't care? *Where does the senseless carnage end?* Could you imagine how much worse it could be if I didn't have a seatbelt on? If there were five people in the car with me, would they be guilty of aiding and abetting? Could we all be charged with a R.I.C.O. violation? No wonder the Great American West was so dangerous 150 years ago, there were no *picture* ID's. And, gasp! No "social security" numbers! (How did the human race survive all those thousands of years without "social security?") This is like those math problems in school everyone hated:

> If person A leaves Chicago at 12:00 without ID traveling at 50 m.p.h. and person B leaves Detroit at 1:00 without ID traveling at 55 m.p.h., at what time are the people in Seattle damaged?

I think the point is made sufficiently. At no point are the

people in Heber, Arizona, affected in any way if I go out to buy raisins (or other dry fruit) without ID in Phoenix. In fact, no one is affected, not even the "cop" who chooses to violently interfere with my life. Now, how does all that square with the political rhetoric commonly called the "Arizona constitution?"

> "Governments derive their just powers from the consent of the governed, and are established to protect and maintain individual rights."—Arizona constitution article II § 2.

It doesn't square with it and no amount of political spin, opinion or violence can make "failure to provide ID" *factually* consistent with this section of Arizona's pretended "supreme law." It then follows that the "constitution" does not "authorize" the actions taken against me. So I ask the "judge" straight out, "are there any allegations of damage here?" More likely than not, if any "duty" is claimed to be breached, then it was "created" by coercion i.e., violence, and there is no damage. No one is damaged by going down the street without a "driver's license" and I have even had "cops" testify that I have not damaged or even *threatened* to damage anyone. And I write "pretended" before "supreme law" because if this clause were complied with bureaucrats could not give out most traffic tickets.

You may be asking yourself, "how would driving down the street *ever* be *safe* again if no one was required to have a driver's license?" I address that issue in the last chapter. Suffice it to say here there are accidents caused every day by "licensed" drivers and no service or product needs to be provided at the barrel of a gun.

Getting back to my "collateral attack" on the so-called "system," a traffic ticket will show there is no victim. So the ticket, *on its face,* is inconsistent with this section of the so-called "constitution." A good question in this regard is: "Did

I violate an individual's rights?" If the answer is no, then the next question is, "would this prosecution be factually consistent with the purpose of the establishment of this government?" In Arizona, it's article II § 2 cited just above.

These questions also apply if I am accused of a so-called "criminal traffic" violation. I just go in with a proposed plea of guilty and let the "judge" know I want to pay the fine and avoid a trial. I just have a few questions I want to ask before paying that fine so I know what is actually going on.

In "criminal" cases, I'm supposed to be informed of the nature and cause of the charges and the proceedings against me. This will usually not happen though. Bureaucrats want money, money they have not earned and they are not interested in fairness. They tend to act as though my alleged right to be informed is a nuisance.

> **Bureaucrats are not in the fairness business. They're in the control, power, and money business. They crave attention, irresponsibility, glory and domination.**

> "To the man who only has a hammer, everything he encounters begins to look like a nail." -- Abraham H. Maslow

Chapter Eight

<u>What role does the "judge" really play?</u>

I usually find this is a good time to question the "judge's" role in all of this. I would say: I understand an armed man dressed in a costume, the "cop," complained about me. However, I am a little unsure about what the "judge" is supposed to do. Why is the "cop" *whining* to this "honorable" lawyer? "Daddy, Marc won't let me see his baseball-your Honor, Marc won't let me see his ID." I will ask the "judge:"

Who do *you* represent in all of this?

I like this question because there's no way out of this particular one for Mr. Wonder Lawyer, the pretended "judge." This is really the *only* question I need to ask to prove the entire proceeding is unfair. It's about as *loaded* a question as there is and he may get *very upset,* and that's fine. The only thing he's accomplishing is throwing his pretense of good faith, fairness and credibility right out the window. I write "there is no way out" because the two points I made above about physical violence and a fair hearing are used here with maximum effect. This question cuts through all of the political window dressing exposing the "trial" for the sham it is, a "sham" in the *lay* sense, of course.

The "judge" will not answer this question and may use it as grounds to claim I'm somehow "refusing to plea." The "judge" would then force me to his political dog and pony show called a "trial" despite my intention to "plead guilty" and pay his "fine." That's why I go in with an unsigned plea of "guilty" (for criminal cases) or a plea of "responsible" (for civil cases). In either case I can ask, "Sir, is that consistent with the facts; there is an unsigned plea of guilty on your bench?" Why not inform me of the *true* nature and cause of the charges and proceedings against me and *then* take my money? This question is loaded because the "judge" has to say one of two things or be non-responsive. Either way, he will have a difficult time maintaining his pretense of fairness.

In the summer of 2002 I helped someone with a "hearing" in Phoenix with individuals calling themselves the "Department of Revenue." The "hearing officer" represented the "director" of the "Department" as did the individual who made the so-called "assessment." Where was the independent and impartial "hearing officer?" There obviously wasn't one. The "hearing" was a joke and was only provided to create the appearance of fairness. Could you imagine a mugger using the same language as a lawyer? He sticks a gun in your face and says, "I've just *assessed* you, now give me your wallet."

This may be the "judge's" first possible response:

A. *He could say he represents no one.* There is almost no chance a "judge" will say he represents no one. However, if he does, then I would ask, "so, you are here on your own authority? A *yes* or *no* will do." Now things start to get really tough for the "judge." The only ways out of this are to throw out this inane "charge" or to start screaming something about "contempt."

What are the implications for an "honorable" lawyer if he claims he is there on his own authority? The premise bureaucrats, such as a "judge," put forth, and *need* to be accepted, is they "represent" the "people" of the "state" as "authorized by the constitution." If he claims he "represents" no one and is there on his own authority, then this false and erroneous premise is destroyed *by his own admission* because...

The "judge" is appearing pursuant to the "constitution" while *not* appearing pursuant to the "constitution."

This particular question undermines any pretense of fairness this violent individual is trying to maintain. The political myth he is a "public servant" is exposed for everyone present as the nonsense it is. This obviously presents a "judge" with a serious "jurisdictional" problem if he is going to claim he is appearing by his own authority. I may ask, "is it your opinion you have "jurisdiction" over me? A yes or no answer will do. "

If he answers no the case is over. This is not likely to happen. A "judge" will usually angrily snap back they do have "jurisdiction." So then I could ask: "Is that an arbitrary legal opinion?" He'll likely say "no" so I can now respond with, "so your legal opinion is based upon facts currently within your knowledge?" Chances are he will say "yes," if not, the case is over. This next question is going to be really tough for the "judge"

> "I'm glad those facts are currently within your knowledge, now, could you please tell me what those facts are and exactly where, when, why and how, *you*, of *your own authority*, actually *acquired* this jurisdiction over me?"

This lawyer cannot *snap* back, "the constitution" without *contradicting* his previous opinion he is not representing anyone. He's stuck. Another important question to ask is: "is your jurisdiction based on my consent?"

The answer I'm looking for is coercion, physical violence. This "judge" has *not* asked for my permission and he will let me know if I ask him questions like this. Because the only answer consistent with reality is "coercion," I can ask him a question that will make him horribly uncomfortable:

> **Do you equate violence and coercion with fairness and good faith?**

There is no way out of the box I've helped put the "judge" in. If he tries to squirm his way out by being non-responsive, I ask: "Tell me, what would happen if I just walked out of here, threw this so-called ticket away, and ignored all of this?" He will probably let me know that some form of physical violence would be used against me such as, a so-called "warrant for my arrest" will be issued. If he doesn't answer I will just ask the above question again or *just walk out.*

By asking what would happen if I turned around and walked away he'll let everyone present know he is prepared to use *physical violence on his own so-called "authority."* This is a pretty bad spot for him to be in. I would then point out he has claimed he is there "on his own authority" and "has acquired jurisdiction by coercion." By *his own admission* his "authority" is violence, not some alleged "delegated authority" from a "constitution." An admission like that would be pretty damaging and is the reason why I will bring witnesses with me and audio recording equipment.

If he is doing all of this by violence, then the question is, can he make an error large enough to "shock the conscience" of any "reviewing" lawyers doing business as an "appellate court?" This raises another interesting question: how do you "shock the conscience" of an individual who relies on violence to acquire property he doesn't own viz., a bureaucrat? He obviously has no respect for human life, so how do you "shock" him? The mere fact that violence *is* his so-called "jurisdiction" should be enough to get *any* case thrown out but, remember, this is not the real world, this is "Legal Land," so it usually doesn't work out that way. In "Legal Land" violence is OK if you have a cool looking badge or a costume on, such as a uniform or a flowing black robe.

If he's there on his own behalf, then, to whom does the "fine" that I pay go? If any money goes to him there is a serious conflict of interest and any pretense of fairness and impartiality goes right out the window once again. And if that money goes to the "state," and the "state" pays him, there is still a conflict of interest. This conflict of interest doesn't magically go away by labeling it the "best system in the world" or sneering "Well, I'd like to see *you* do better Marc."

This is why there is *never* any impartiality in any so-called "tax" case. All bureaucrats are paid by money "stolen" (*lay* sense) from pretended "taxpayers." Therefore, the "judge" in any "tax" case has a financial interest in each and every case that comes through. Impartiality and independence is a cruel joke.

You should also consider the political nonsense the "state" is everyone in a certain geographic location. This would obviously include the "honorable" lawyer with the neat robe. How could one of the very people *tragically* damaged by my reckless act of traveling without ID also sit as a "judge?" Where's the independence?

If the "judge" is there on his own behalf, then what does this say about his *relationship* to the "cop" who came in crying about someone not having a seatbelt on? *Why is the "cop" whining to him, what is his motive*? I could really put this "judge" on the spot by holding up the ticket and asking him, "What is the nature and basis of your relationship with this "cop" who filed this alleged complaint against me?" If he has no relationship with him, *then why is he taking control over my life and my property of his own "authority" for him*? There is obviously some kind of relationship going on here. At the very least, there is some kind of business relationship . I think that would qualify as a conflict of interest. This line of questioning could really expose the "judge" and show, "beyond a reasonable doubt," there is only a thin pretense of fairness going on here.

I know some people, especially *lawyers*, would complain and allege their "adversary system" is the "best system in the world." My response to that is, "Yeah, right, great logic." What a *strong argument* in *favor* of violence and *sham* "trials" that lawyers, by the way, have a "vested" interest in supporting and perpetuating by assisting the pretended "state" in *your* prosecution, ***by acting as your "judge," or by "helping" to "protect" you from the other two lawyers in the courtroom.*** Get it? Your life, honesty and fairness are just not as important as a their next house, car or boat. I understand that "federal" minimum security *prisons* are much better than "state" maximum security *prisons*, but that doesn't mean I want to go to federal prison. A prison is still a prison for goodness sake. "What about Hawaii this year honey?" "Are you kidding me? Have you seen this brochure for the federal prison?"

Let's say there is an "election" going on here in Arizona and one guy is running for "attorney general." His "platform" is that he's the "most qualified." Now that's pretty misleading isn't it? In a class of idiots, a few are bound to be at *the head* of the class right? But even the best and the brightest among a class of idiots are still considered idiots, aren't they?

Now let's take a close look at the "judge's" second possible response:

B. *He could say he represents the "state" or the "people" of the "state."* This, the more likely answer he might give, *if any at all*, presents the "judge" with a different, though, just as deep hole to dig himself out of. Like my last question, there is no way for this lawyer to answer without destroying whatever pretense of fairness, good faith and impartiality he was lucky enough to have had up until this point.

The "judge" is supposed to be an independent, fair and impartial decision-maker. Not in my opinion, but according to the BS public relations bureaucrats continually spew forth. There is a serious contradiction here though; if he represents the "state," or the alleged "people" of the "state," then he also represents the alleged complaining party and the "cop," who also just happens to claim to represent the "state!" Under his own rules a fair trial is still impossible.

> **Bureaucrats are so compulsive about making rules they fail to see those very same rules completely hamstring their jobs if applied.**

Here the "judge" also represents the "cop" who filed the "complaint" (traffic ticket, summons, etc.) in the first place. This fact is repeatedly demonstrated throughout this book in the way the "judge" continually comes to the aid and defense of the "cop" each and every time I try to get down to the brass tacks truth. I would therefore ask the "judge" if he does in fact represent the "cop." This sets the "judge" up to contradict himself when he assumes the "cop's" burden of proof.

After admitting he "represents" the "state," I would ask, "Sir, are you telling me you *represent* the alleged *complaining party*?" If he says "no," I ask him to clarify his position:

> **Please explain how you can represent the "state" and *not* represent the "state" at the very same time.**

This is classic "Legal Land" nonsense. In "Legal Land," a so-called "judge" can represent the "state" and *not* represent the "state" at the *very same time*. In the real world such a person is called a charlatan, crook, swindler, con man, rogue etc. But, in "Legal Land" he is hailed as a scholar, given a small army at his disposal, and relieved of any and all personal responsibility or liability. Just check your local "judge's" "ethics" rules. In all probability, there is absolutely no criminal or civil liability attached to their "errors."

> In "Legal Land" "judges" do not commit *crimes;* no these "honorable" lawyers commit *errors* – just a "harmless error" even if you spend time in prison getting gang-raped.

"Judges" only have their fellow "judges" looking over their shoulders who, themselves, determine what discipline is to be exercised against any one "judge" that someone may have complained about, if any. They call this "sovereign" or "judicial immunity." It sure feels good to be the "king" doesn't it?

Another question is this: "Sir, seeing how you represent the alleged complaining party as well, could you please explain *where, when, why* and *how* I'm supposed to get a fair trial under these circumstances?" I may also ask *when* the impartial decision-maker intends on appearing and why the plaintiff's (the "state's") lawyer is conducting the so-called "arraignment." I would also ask why the plaintiff (the "state") requires two lawyers. I then remind the "judge" I'm not a lawyer and don't want a trial, I just want to pay the fine. But, before doing so, I just want to know what is going on before I pay. Unless of course informing me of the nature and cause of the charges and proceedings is a nuisance.

If he still refuses, I ask him, "why should I enter a plea when there is no evidence of a complaining party and you will not answer a few simple questions and inform me of the nature and basis of the charges and proceedings against me?" The "judge" will not be able to maintain any consistency with such questions. If he refuses to answer who he represents, I ask who pays him. The "judge" wants, no *needs* to make it look as if the "constitution," an unsigned "written instrument" allows him to hold me there against my will. *As if a piece of paper can authorize anything*. **Paper and ink does not authorize anything, <u>people do</u>**. This is why the contention the constitution is binding on anyone is absurd. The paper and ink is only to record their will and intentions. Notwithstanding that, such a position is consistent with his opinion he represents the "state," and, here, the "state" is also the alleged complaining party! This lawyer represents both the "state" and the pretended plaintiff, the alleged complaining party, the same so-called "state." Get it?

In the real world, this is not called justice. This is called crazy or just plain nuts.

Not only is this "nuts," but this presents a serious conflict of interest under their own so-called "ethical" "rules" (if you can even imagine, for a moment, that a so-called "judge" actually *has* any ethical rules under these bizarre circumstances, enumerated both above, and below):

A. *There is no independence.* "Judicial independence" is a very popular myth; there has never been an independent judiciary in U.S. courts. If the "judge" represents the plaintiff, then this is inconsistent with his *ethics* code mandating independence: "An independent and honorable judiciary is indispensable to justice in our society." Arizona Rules of the Supreme Court, Rule 81, Canon 1.

B. *There is impropriety.* This is obvious: "A judge shall respect and comply with the law and shall act at all times in a manner that promotes public confidence in the integrity and impartiality of the judiciary." Canon 2. This is ridiculous for several reasons. The "judge's" own rules permit him to "suspend" whatever rules he wants, such as appellate rule 3 in Arizona. Another is the violence. How is confidence promoted by violence? Yes, I'm *confident* this "honorable" lawyer will have me killed if I don't play along with his fantasies. Last, where is the impartiality when the "judge" is a complaining party?

C. *There is no impartiality.* Again, this is obvious: "A judge shall perform the duties of judicial office impartially and diligently." Canon 3. This is impossible when he represents *both* the pretended plaintiff and also the defendant at certain times.

D. *There is no disqualification.* This is a big one and I will quote much of their "canon" here:

> "A judge shall disqualify himself or herself in a proceeding in which the judge's impartiality might reasonably be questioned, including but not limited to instances where:

> The judge has a personal bias or prejudice concerning a party or a party's lawyer, or personal knowledge of disputed evidentiary facts concerning the proceeding;
>
> The ***judge served as a lawyer in the matter in controversy***, or a lawyer with whom the judge practiced law within the proceeding seven (7) years served during such association as a lawyer concerning the matter, or the judge has been a material witness concerning it..." Canon 3(E) (emphasis mine).

Now, I'm no *lawyer*, but a "judge" representing the plaintiff (the "state"), is a conflict of interest, at least in the lay sense. The "judge's" representation of the pretended plaintiff is acting as a lawyer and is precluded by their own rules. Not to worry though, this is "Legal Land" so the rules, even those that *specifically* apply to the "judges," *don't really apply*. They are only P.R., public relations to *dupe* you, for pretense.

> **Yes, the rules apply and they *don't* apply at the same time.**

The "judge's" representation of the "plaintiff" destroys any perception or illusion of fairness and, fortunately their victims don't have to go to "law school" in order to see that. This also "violates" at least four (4) of their own ethics rules and that doesn't include their "statutes" and "constitutions." And here, I was only being accused of not providing ID? Remember the old lollipop commercial? How many crimes does an "honorable" lawyer have to commit to "convict" someone of not carrying ID?

This brings us back to what was written earlier with regards to "the Rule of Necessity." The commentary for this rule includes:

> By decisional law, the rule of necessity may override the rule of disqualification.

Whenever bureaucrats *feel* it's "necessary" to disregard their own ethics rules *they will do so* even if this means failing to disqualify themselves over any cause over which their impartiality might reasonably be questioned. Would that be legal anarchy? And, as we have seen, this happens all the time. Yes, in their "legal" minds it is absolutely *necessary* to deny me any pretense of fairness so they can steal (*lay* sense) my money and valuable time. Here we can see their very own "commentary" on their very own "ethics" rules makes it perfectly clear:

> ***You* are *going* to stand trial whether that trial is fair or not and, whether you like it, or not.**

As we can see, this has nothing to do with "fairness," and everything to do with taking control of my life, liberty and property using whatever violence and subterfuge a lawyer thinks is "necessary." It's all about control. It's all about obedience.

No *rational* lay individual could read the "judge's" own commentary on "necessity" and still claim there is a "government of laws, not men." Unless of course laughter is their objective. Lawyers can and will claim there is a "government of laws, not men," because lawyers will have you believe anything. That's their job; *even if the lawyer himself does not personally believe the nonsense he is trying to put over on you.* I have spoken to many lawyers and know this to be true. One in particular works for the so-called "attorney general" in California. This lawyer told me he would defend a "revenue agent's" actions that were contrary to *his professional legal advice.* Let me clarify: this lawyer could advise his client *not* to do something because the act was *illegal.* If the agent disregarded the "official legal advice" of his lawyer and was then sued by the person consequently damaged, then this lawyer would *defend the very actions he advised against.*

If they want to render an honest legal opinion for a change, what the "honorable" lawyers parading around as "courts of justice" should say is this:

> **You are entitled to a fair hearing but only *if* we feel like granting one. By the way, *we never do;* we can't.**

As we can now see, these rules, *if applied,* make it *impossible* for an honest "judge" to conduct a traffic case or any criminal case for that matter. This is yet another example of where bureaucrats, in their zeal to ram rules down everyone *else's* throats, hamstring themselves right out of a job.

> **Bureaucrats cannot follow their own rules and still function.**

After all, here, the "judge" represents the plaintiff for goodness sake, so the trial *cannot* possibly be fair. In fact, it isn't proper to call it a trial at all; it's a joke, a sham or a charade, but not a trial. A trial is essentially a *test* and nothing is tested except for the patience of all involved. *Calling it a "trial" is a lie.* There is another "legal" term for this; it's called a kangaroo court.

If the "judge" insists on proceeding further, as he usually will, I could ask, "Does the complaining party have standing to complain" and, if he says, "yes," then I could ask, "How and why?" The "judge" could refuse to answer. I would then ask: "O.K., is there a cause of action here to plea to?" He'll probably confidently say there is. I would then respond, "O.K., I'm not agreeing or disagreeing but, could you tell me the elements of a cause of action?" What makes the "judge" so sure? If he is sure, then he must know what those elements are. He's so confident not because there's evidence of a cause of action, but because there's a battery of armed men waiting in the wings to carry me off to jail on a moment's notice, men that do not exercise any discretion of their own.

However, no amount of violence changes what a "cause of action" is, or is *supposed to be.* Putting me in jail does not reverse "supreme court" opinions as far as I know. A "cause of action" is a breach of a known "legal" duty that results in loss, harm or injury. There are many cases showing this. The following is only one from the "United States Supreme Court"

> "Like the prudential component, the constitutional component of standing doctrine incorporates concepts concededly not susceptible of precise definition. ***The injury alleged must be, for example," 'distinct and palpable,'"*** Gladstone, Realtors v. Village of Bellwood, 441 U.S. 91, 100 (1979) (quoting Warth v. Seldin, supra, at 501), and ***not "abstract" or "conjectural" or "hypothetical,"*** Los Angeles v. Lyons, 461 U.S. 95, 101-102 (1983); O'Shea v. Littleton, 414 U.S. 488, 494 (1974). ***The injury must be "fairly" traceable to the challenged action, and relief from the injury must be "likely" to follow from a favorable decision.*** See Simon v. Eastern Kentucky Welfare Rights Org., 426 U.S., at 38, 41." *Allen v. Wright,* 468 U.S. 737 (1984) (emphasis mine).
>
> And, from Arizona:
>
> "[it] is equally true that before one is entitled to a remedy against an alleged wrongdoer, ***there must be some duty owing from the wrongdoer towards the injured person.***" *State Compensation Fund v. Superior Court,* 15 Ariz.App. 597, 598, 490 P.2d 426 (1972) (emphasis mine).

I may ask the judge: "Is this cause of action factually consistent with the Supreme Court's opinion as to what a cause of action is?" If he says yes, I then ask him if he can tell me what facts are before him to support such an opinion and who presented them.

There is no damage done because I travel without a "license," ID or other picture card in my pocket. A "license" may even have been issued to me, but just because I leave it at home does not mean there is damage or a *prejudice* to the rights of another man, woman or child. I guess we all walk a fine (legal) line between being an innocent person and a vicious, heinous criminal who deserves to rot in a cage for six months.

The quotes from the above cited court cases are pretty clear. Not only must there be damage, but that damage "must be 'fairly' traceable to the challenged action, and relief from the injury must be 'likely' to follow from a favorable decision." Here we can see yet again the "laws" imposed on us at the barrel of a gun just don't apply to bureaucrats because, in this particular case, "by *decisional* law, the rule of necessity may override the rule of standing." Obviously, this is not fair. There is no injury to people in Parker, Arizona if I don't have ID on me while in Tucson so maybe the lawyers who wrote the above opinion *actually* meant to write:

> [it] is equally true that before one is entitled to a remedy against an alleged wrongdoer, **there must be some duty owing from the wrongdoer towards the injured person, except for individuals pretending to be the state, where no such standards exists; the state has standing against anyone that falls within its sights**.

The issue of standing is *supposed* to be very important, just ask a lawyer. The complaining party is *supposed* to have standing to complain. Without standing anyone can sue anyone else for anything. It's common sense there must be something to complain about with that complaint coming from someone who actually has the right to complain.

Although bureaucrats ignore standing whenever they are the so-called "plaintiff," it is their *first line of defense* whenever a complaint is made against *them.* Isn't that ironic? File a complaint against a bureaucrat and their first well-rehearsed reaction is to file a copy and pasted motion to dismiss "for failure to state a claim" or for a "lack of jurisdiction." In California it's called a "demurrer." I know they are copies because they do not always change all the names.

Thus, another question designed to undermine the false perception of fairness they try so hard to put over is:

What is the nature of the relationship, if any, between us?

This question really gets to the heart of the matter and is similar to the questions on "jurisdiction." Either the "judge" answers it or he doesn't. **I don't care either way because both work against him**. In fact, any answer at all destroys any pretended case this bureaucrat is trying to put over. If he doesn't answer he's demonstrating bad faith because he's refusing to inform me of the nature of the proceeding so I can defend myself. That's unfair even in the "legal" sense. If he does answer, it will be revealed that this "relationship" is based on his coercion and threats of violence. I can then ask if he equates coercion with good faith. If he refuses to answer, I tell him I'll be asking the "cop" the same question, that is, what is the nature of the relationship between me and the pretended "judge." After all, his crying about me not having an ID card in my pocket started this mess; he filed the so-called "complaint" and is supposed to have the burden of proving "jurisdiction." I also tell him by refusing to inform me of the nature of the proceedings I cannot possibly defend myself.

It stands to reason if there is no relationship I should be able to walk away from "his" courtroom and not have to worry about any further aggression and violence. Because of this, I may ask, "am I free to walk away without any further aggression?" If not, I ask why. Sooner or later the true nature of the "relationship" will be revealed by his words or actions and it will not be consistent with any *rational* sense of fairness. A common thief points a gun at you and says, "your money or your life," and a "judge" essentially says the same thing except for the fluffy political lingo, "you appear in my courtroom or I'll issue a bench warrant for your immediate arrest."

All of this is geared towards exposing the true nature of what is happening, no political opinions, no deletion, distortion or adding to reality, just the facts. Most dealings with bureaucrats are based upon violence so they usually do their best to cover it up, *to a point*. Some will admit to it, although they may also claim it is a "last resort." Great excuse, most criminals would also say the same thing. It's probably true that criminals would probably not use violence, or nearly as much violence, if their victims ("citizens," "residents") simply rolled over and complied with their demands. Can you imagine how that would look as a so-called "law?"

> A.R.S. § 13-1105. *First degree murder; classification*
>
> A. A person commits first degree murder if:
>
> 1. Intending or knowing that the person's conduct will cause death, the person causes the death of another with premeditation, ***unless it is done as a "last resort" by a bureaucrat.***

To illustrate violence is the *modus operandi* ("M.O.") of bureaucrats, just imagine what compliance would be like if they could not use violence. Or, rather, let's look at how "easy" their "jobs" would still be if they weren't *helped* out by their victims.

Maybe it's just me, but isn't it the height of arrogance to not ask permission while asking for help?

Who would pull their cars over to the side of the road if the "cops" weren't bent on using violence ("by any means necessary") to get your car to stop? Would anyone even appear in court if there were no violent mechanism to force you to be there? "Sir, please come to court with me *please*. If you don't show up we cannot fine you and the judge will not get paid."

How could the shameless assault and robbery going under the political spin "eminent domain" be accomplished *except* by violence? To demonstrate bureaucrats operate by violence and have no respect for human life, I'll cite one of their *own* opinions:

> "Hence, although the goal of extinguishing aboriginal title could have been achieved by congressional fiat, see *Tee-Hit-Ton Indians v. United States,* 348 US 272, 279 1955)." *Idaho v. United States et al.* on writ of certiorari to the United States court of appeals for the ninth circuit [June 18, 2001].

"Extinguishing…title?" *Who talks like that*? What does that mean? It means, "you're not the owner anymore, we are." Does it look like the lawyers of the "Supreme Court" have respect for human life or the property they lie about "protecting?" This opinion is political gibberish for robbery, the taking of property by force and without the owner's consent.

> **No, your Honor, this guy's nuts, I didn't car-jack him, I just "extinguished" his title to the car, that's all, I swear.**

These lawyers also write title to property could have

been "achieved by congressional fiat." This is more political window dressing I will break down.

First, congress is a group of men and women. Second, "fiat" is defined as: "an order or decree." *Oxford American Dictionary*, Page 320. What these lawyers are saying is that title to property (ownership) can be acquired by the mere *say-so* of a group of 535 men and women. Some men and women (congress) just have to say it's theirs and POOF! it's *magically* theirs. A little political voodoo and sleight of hand and it's done. "What wonderful magic" indeed. If you think I'm being harsh or too critical here, then consider the fact the lawyers D/B/A the "Supreme Court" refer to their very own "law" as "wonderful magic"

> "We must comment upon the final paragraphs of Part II of the concurrences opinion which bring on stage, in classic fashion, a *deus ex machina* to extract, from the seemingly insoluble difficulties that the prior writing has created, a happy ending. The concurrence manages to have its cake and eat it too to hand over state law-enforcement officers to the jurisdiction of tribal courts and yet still assure that the officers traditional immunity (and hence the States law-enforcement interest) will be protected by simply announcing that in order to protect government officials, immunity defenses should be considered in reviewing tribal court jurisdiction. *Post*, at 16 (opinion of *O'Connor*, J.). ***What wonderful magic***." *Nevada et al. v. Hicks et al.* certiorari to the united states court of appeals for the ninth circuit No. 991994. Argued March 21, 2001, Decided June 25, 2001 (***bold italics*** mine).

Wow...and, to think, when I want property that doesn't

belong me, I actually *pay for it* or rent it from the owner; in other words, I only do so with the owner's freely given consent. Pretty radical and extreme concept. ***It's called trade.*** And by the way, the "functions of a public office" are defined as a "trade or business" under the "Internal Revenue Code" at section 7701(26). How's that for a bold-faced lie? What is being "traded" when the "IRS" attacks you? Your money for their sparing your life, that's what.

Who would have ever thought that I could just "decree" a particular piece of property is mine and thereby avoid having to pay for it? I had no idea I possessed such an awesome power to do that, and, to think of it, apparently we *all* do. Well, that's the *political* theory bureaucrats desperately want us to *believe* anyway. Bureaucrats would have us believe the lie that "congress" (a group of men and women) exercises a so-called "delegated authority." Well, if "congress" has the "authority" to just "decree" property is theirs, then they must gave gotten this awesome power from somewhere or someone else. The theory or opinion is that this pretended "authority" comes from "We the People..." This is a myth as silly as the so-called "divine right of kings." It's one thing to claim God gave you the right to dominate other men, women and children, but, to claim the person you are *dominating* gave you the right? Who would *freely* volunteer to be dominated by another?

O.K., I know if I "decree" my neighbor's car to be mine and then I take it, without their consent, then I'm a car thief and a nitwit to boot, right? And that's true even if I believe it's "necessary" for me to have that car, correct? That would mean I lack this awesome super-human power doesn't it? I'm pretty sure my neighbor has no "authority" to do that either. After all, what would be the point of robbery "statutes" if this were not true? Now, if *I* lack the authority, then *I* cannot delegate what *I* don't have to anyone, even a so-called "congressman."

Using the simple rules of mathematics, we can therefore eliminate any so-called "*collective*" right to commit robbery, after all, if my neighbor and I lack that power or "authority," then we gain nothing by getting together and forming a *gang* called a "congress" do we? The simple mathematical principal the whole is equal to the sum of its part applies here. If my neighbor and I have one rock each, together we only have two, not 1000, as politicians would have us believe.

Now, just imagine someone going into court and using the same "legal" reasoning (defense) bureaucrats use to justify their taking of property by force, such as in the case of a car-jacking:

> "I'm not guilty your Honor."
>
> "And why is that?"
>
> "Because, the rule of necessity overrode that jerk's property rights; it was *necessary* for me to have his car and his title was *extinguished*."
>
> "You're right, would you like me to sanction the previous owner for harassing you with this patently frivolous complaint?"

This isn't really a joke though. It's the so-called "adversary system" being portrayed as a system of justice that's a joke. The joke is also on those who take it seriously. After all, if the so-called "authority" that is *allegedly* delegated to the men and women called the "government" is from the people, then the people themselves *must* possess this awesome power, right? But do they? Do they really have a "collective right" to commit armed robbery? *Do you think you have a collective right to steal*? If you lack the right, then anybody pretending to "represent" you lacks the right.

If the people do have a collective right to steal, then *nothing* would be a crime and the need for a so-called "government" would be gone. After all, if anything can be done out of some mere opinion that it's "necessary," then there are no "rights" to be protected. In that case, the Nazi's hung at Nuremberg may have used the wrong legal defense. Instead of arguing "we were just following orders," they could have taken a clue from bureaucrats here and argued, "by *decisional* law (Hitler's opinion), the rule of *necessity* overrode the right of any Jew (or other "enemy") to life, liberty and property." Do you see how crazy this sounds?

In fact, another gross contradiction is the "legal" opinion politicians hold that their "legal" right to commit armed robbery is "superior" to the very rights they claim to be "protecting"

> "The power of eminent domain ... is superior to property rights (Kohl v. United States, 91 U.S. 367, 371)..." *State of Ga. v. City of Chattanooga*, 264 U.S. 472, 480 (1924).

In the bureaucratic fantasy world I call "Legal Land," non-bureaucrats (the productive) do not <u>own</u> *anything*. After all, what *is* an owner?

> "**owner.** One who has complete dominion over particular property. 42 Am J1st Prop § 37." *Ballentine's Law Dictionary*, page 906.

Stripped of lawyerese and political gibberish, the lawyers D/B/A a "Supreme Court" are saying the power to *steal* property "is superior" to the right to *own* property or

> "The power of ***armed robbery*** ... is superior to property rights (Kohl v. United States, 91 U.S. 367, 371)..." *State of Ga. v. City of Chattanooga*, 264 U.S. 472, 480 (1924) (my edits in ***bold italics***).

Do you have "complete dominion" over everything you *think* you own? Well, *think again*. In "Legal Land" you don't, you own nothing, not even the shirt on your back. *And even your shirt has to be worn in the manner some bureaucrat prescribes.* As it turns out, in the minds of lawyers and bureaucrats "We the people" don't really *own* anything because "the power of eminent domain...is superior to property rights." Yes, that's right, the power to *steal* is "superior" to individual property rights (which as we'll see later, don't even exist in the minds of bureaucrats). And from where was this awesome "delegated" power acquired? That's right, it's mere *fiat* (order or decree), **because some "honorable" lawyers <u>said so</u>**, that's why. Silly me, I thought bureaucrats were supposed to *protect* property. Maybe "protect" is a "word of art" and in the *legal* sense means to steal.

> "The people have always some champion whom they set over them and nurse into greatness. This and no other is the root from which a tyrant springs; when he first appears he is a protector." -Plato.

Let's use an analogy here to further illustrate what these politicians are saying. You bring some of your valuable property to a private storage facility. After paying the agreed upon price for temporary storage, you come back a few months later and all your stuff is gone. You ask the owner about it and he tells you he took and sold it all, and, by the way, the price increased *retroactively* so now you must also pay more money before you are permitted to leave. You must also pay for the *next* six months because your account is now considered in "jeopardy." If not, then he'll "seize [your] bank accounts."

You ask him why he sold your valuables and he tells you, "my right to take it is superior to your property rights." He might even say:

> "By *decisional* law, the rule of necessity overrode your property rights."

As opposed to bureaucrats, at least you would not be *compelled* to keep putting valuables in that guy's place. However, could you imagine how insane such a situation would be? In fact, the situation with bureaucrats is far worse because, as I just wrote, they don't believe individual "citizens" own *anything*. They only acknowledge the statist nonsense and fantasy that *bureaucrats own everything*:

> "The ultimate ownership of all property is in the State; individual so-called "ownership" is only by virtue of Government, i.e., law, amounting to mere user; and that use must be in accordance with law and subordinate to the necessities of the State." *Senate Resolution #62*, from April 1933.

Keep in mind this is not my opinion nor was it written by Karl Marx or any other prominent communists. It's the so-called "law of the land." Reread that last part; that means a bureaucrat believes he has the right to dictate the way you brush your teeth. And there is that word *necessity* again. "Necessity has no law..." *Ballentine's Law Dictionary*, page 837. Wow, how does that square with the part about the "law" above? In part this means the "law" applies to everyone, except bureaucrats.

All of this raises a very interesting question. Remember the question that plagued us in early childhood, "which came first, the chicken or the egg?"

> **Which came first, individual property rights, or the so-called "government?"**

Can you imagine what these "senators" were like as children? If another kid asked a future "senator" to play in his sandbox, did the "senator" stand up declaring, "OK, I'll play in your sandbox. But, this is now *my* sandbox and you can only use it in the manner I allow you. If not, you will *all* be held in *contempt*!"

This opinion by the "senate" is the *mother* of what lawyers call a "non sequitur," which means: "It does not follow." *Ballentine's Law Dictionary*, page 862. This opinion does not mean I am *not* the owner of my property. This only means there are men and women among us who have no respect for human life *refusing to recognize* I do own property. At least a mugger realizes your money isn't his. He says, "*your* money or *your* life." Brimming with the supreme self-confidence that only comes from believing you are an exalted "sovereign," bureaucrats say, "*our* money or *your* life." Now I ask you, which is worse?

There was once a time when many refused to believe the earth was round, but that belief didn't make the earth any less round. If someone wants to deny parts of reality that's his business. *Thinking* I'm the Easter Bunny doesn't make me the Easter Bunny and my delusion doesn't interfere with your life. Just because somebody pays me to dress up and play Santa Claus doesn't mean I am Santa Claus. The same is true if a man is paid to pretend to be a "judge." The problem is some individuals insist on backing their delusions with violence. When that happens, we are forced to accept, or to act upon, both negative hallucinations, and in a sense *halluci-**Nations***, as well as positive ones, imposed upon us by bureaucrats. One such negative hallucination is that individual property rights do not exist while a positive one is that *corporations* somehow do exist.

Again, the Arizona constitution boasts:

> "Governments derive their just powers from the consent of the governed, and are established to protect and maintain individual rights." — Arizona constitution article II § 2.

The word "derive" means the people and their rights

exist *prior* to the creation of a so-called "state," if such a thing even exists. As we have seen it does not. This is a serious problem for bureaucrats. The "senate" and "supreme court" hold the opinion the people have no property rights without the wonderful, benevolent, superhuman men and women prancing around calling themselves a "government." What rights did people have to protect in the first place when they allegedly created the "state?" If the people have no property rights, as the "senate" asserts, then why would they need to have a "state" in the first place? *There is nothing to protect*! Conversely, if they did have those rights, then somewhere down the line bureaucrats refused to accept this particular part of reality. In either case, there is nothing to protect! As we can now see:

> **Bureaucrats argue themselves right out of a job.**

As I have said before, "don't bring a knife to a gunfight." Know *who* you are dealing with. Bureaucrats, through their own actions and legal opinions demonstrate they not only have no respect for human life, but are also extremely hostile towards the reality people have rights at all. Knowing this I can frame questions so they will expose themselves for what they are.

Back to the relationship between the "judge" and myself. If the "judge" gets upset, threatens me and calls security; then he's just proving, by his own actions, the "relationship" is based on violence, and actions *always* speak louder than words. If this happens, then I always like to ask "Are you threatening me with physical violence for doing nothing more than asking you a few simple questions?"

I sometimes wonder if these "judges" are this violent *outside* of "their" courtrooms when there are no armed men ready to carry out their "orders?" What happens if they are eating dinner in a restaurant and the waitress forgets to bring them a cup of coffee? Do they start screaming they'll have the waitress held in *contempt* if she doesn't get that cup of coffee *fast enough*? When she brings the bill does he refuse to pay her by claiming the charge is "legally defective" or a "nullity" because she's not "licensed" to serve "honorable" lawyers? Also, as "cops" wear their costumes all the time, *picture* a "judge" wearing his robe while walking down the street on his lunch break. Could a hot dog vendor hand a hot dog *directly* to the "judge," or would he have to hand it to his "bailiff" who would then hand it to the "judge?"

At this point, I would ask the "judge" again, "*do you equate physical violence with good faith, yes or no*?" This is really the heart of the matter. There is no way out of questions like these except to be non-responsive and that is why so many typewritten court "orders" offer absolutely no explanation for a "judge's" so-called "decision." Instead, their "order" will only read, "MOTION TO DISMISS: DENIED." When a "judge" has no grounds for his decision he won't give any. Why else would they fall silent? I had a "judge " give a three minute discourse explaining why he refused to permit a court reporter into the court. However, he then vehemently refused to provide any grounds to support his decision allowing a lawyer to appear unchallenged.

This is true even when you notify the "judge" *in advance* that you will *need* an explanation if your request is denied so the "higher" court "judges" can have something to review instead of mere silence:

> "While district court's decision to seal court documents is reviewed only for abuse of discretion, it is imperative that district court articulate its reasons for electing to seal or not to seal a record; ***without full explanation, Court of Appeals is unable to review the district court's exercise of its discretion.***" *E.E.O.C. v. National Children's Center*, 98 F.3d 1406, 1407 (D.C. Cir. 1996) (emphasis mine).

The "law" means nothing to "judges" and has never stopped them from refusing to give a basis for their decisions. One example is found in the Arizona constitution: "Justice in all cases shall be administered openly..." Article II § 11. So when a "judge" sneers at me he "doesn't have to provide his grounds," I know he cares not a whit for the very "law" he took a feigned oath to uphold and comply with. I've also had clerks and "judicial assistants" tell me "judges" do not have to provide any grounds for their decisions. It's great to be the king. Could you imagine a *mechanic* doing that? Visualize getting a three thousand-dollar bill after bringing your car in for an oil change. You ask the mechanic what he is charging you for and he refuses to tell you; pay the bill or you don't get your car back. You tell his co-worker and he snaps, "He's the mechanic, he doesn't have to give you a reason." I would suggest that if it's dishonest for a mechanic to do that, then it's just as dishonest for a lawyer to do the same. Also, consider a doctor charging you for an additional operation and refusing to tell you what he did to you.

Some may argue you could complain to the "Better Business Bureau" about such a mechanic. I agree, but who do you complain to if a "judge" does the same thing? To other "judges." You stay in the same vicious circle with lawyers who just don't care.

Truth does not involve nonsensical legalese double talk and no amount of "Supreme Court" rhetoric, dictum, fiat, or other forms of "legal" mumbo jumbo would be responsive when I ask if he equates violence with good faith. A simple yes or no is all that is required to be responsive.

Another problem for the "judge" is that being non-responsive also destroys his pretense of fairness and credibility. In America you are *supposed* to have the "right" to be informed of the nature and cause of the charges and proceedings against you, at least, allegedly, and he is refusing to be responsive and answer a few simple questions. That's easy enough, isn't it? If I am not informed, then how can I possibly defend myself? What if, on the other hand, I hire one of his fellow lawyers? A full *bar* member, just like him, will he *then* finally answer my questions? If he will only answer in that event then I would have a case for bias and prejudice against me, a mere non-lawyer, and in favor of my representative, Mr. Lawyer.

The problem is, at least in my experience, no lawyer will ask questions like this because they would then be stripped of their pretended "license" to "practice law." Or maybe they are just afraid they will be "disbarred." This is because they would be exposing the fact their entire "system" is a *sham*. This may help to explain why your "friendly" lawyer is required to "take and subscribe an oath to support" the constitutions and "laws of the state" before getting their "license" to "practice law" in the first place. To join in on the racket, you must pledge your support to that racket. This is why lawyers have told me I would be "disbarred" if I were a lawyer. If enough lawyers (and non-lawyers) were to start challenging and questioning the philosophical and political underpinnings of the entire "adversary system" with a few questions like the one's described in this book, then the whole thing might *finally* come crashing down.

Trying to get to the bottom of anything in a courtroom, especially *the truth,* is like working on an "X-File" because *so much* appears hidden and *nothing* is ever as it appears to be.

I am *not* required "by law" to have a lawyer "represent" me in order to be fully informed as to the true nature and cause of the charge and the proceedings against me. If I have a "right" to defend myself this includes being informed as to what is *really* going on. However, and here's the beauty of this, the "judge" cannot inform me as to the nature of the proceedings against me without contradicting his pretense of fairness.

Typically, the "judge" will get ticked off with me by this point and will enter a "plea" for me. If he does, great; I can really put him on the spot, by asking, "despite my own proposed plea of guilty, you just entered a plea for me, are you now representing me?" This question is not intended to be sarcastic or "disrespectful" to the "judge" in any way. It's merely a logical and reasonable question to ask because he entered a plea for me, even though I have a proposed plea of guilty *sitting right on his bench.* To really see the lunacy in this, picture a salesman acting the same way. I am interested in purchasing the product if it can do what he claims it can do. I just want it demonstrated *first.* Instead of demonstrating the product and getting my money, he starts screaming at me for not being interested in his product and "playing games." Such an imbecile isn't going to win any sales awards.

Once again, this demonstrates that all traffic proceedings and courts in general have nothing to do with consent or anything the "defendant" says or does. Appearance at any "trial" enables bureaucrats to maintain their pretense of fairness but it's still just an illusion:

> See, he had his day in court. No, he could not defend himself competently, we were uncooperative, non-responsive and argumentative, but, he was *there physically in* the courtroom, and we treat *everyone* else the same way so he received due process and equal protection under the law.

Oddly enough, as we have seen, even though the "Supreme Court" is extremely hostile to individual property rights and human life in general, they nonetheless hold the opinion a hearing must be held "at a meaningful time and in *a meaningful manner.* Armstrong v. Manzo, 380 U.S. 545, 552 (1965)." *Goldberg v. Kelly*, 397 U.S. 254, 268 (1970) (emphasis mine). By quoting this, or other opinions, I am not implying the "Supreme Court" actually *believes* what they write or they expect other "courts" to be consistent with their opinions. I'm only demonstrating the inconsistencies.

How "meaningful" a hearing is it when my questions have been ignored? How "meaningful" a hearing is it when it's based on violence as demonstrated by the fact the "judge" clearly refuses to respect that I am a human being in full possession of individual property rights? How "meaningful" a hearing is it when, in the opinion of lawyers, I am *incapable* of defending myself?

Another blatant inconsistency from the lawyers doing business as the "Supreme Court" is where they write about the exercise of jurisdiction, in particular, that it should *not*:

> "offend 'traditional notions of fair play and substantial justice.'" International Shoe Co. v. Washington, supra, at 316, quoting Milliken v. Meyer, 311 U.S. 457, 463 (1940)." *World-Wide Volkswagen Corp. v. Woodson*, 444 U.S. 286, 292 (1980).

Excuse me, I'm no lawyer, but, when did *rational* people start believing violence does not, itself, offend "traditional notions of fair play and substantial justice?" To put the question differently, if violence does not offend "traditional notions of fair play and substantial justice," then *what does*? "Legally defective" truth, i.e., anything outside of "Legal Land" offends "traditional notions of fair play and substantial justice."

The exercise of "jurisdiction" itself is an act of violence that *unquestionably* offends "traditional notions of fair play and substantial justice," unless, of course, the lawyers who wrote that opinion meant to somehow *exclude* violence at the hands of their fellow bureaucrats. In that case, it is perfectly O.K.

If all we did was look at the actions of bureaucrats and change their D/B/A or alter ego name from the "City of Sacramento" to "Rizzo's Raisin Company," we would have no problem seeing the act of taking control over a person's life, liberty and property to be an act of violence that offends any and all "traditional notions of fair play and substantial justice," however denominated. If taking control of someone else's life, liberty and property coercively does *not* "offend traditional notions of fair play and substantial justice," then what else is left for a "judge" to do during a "trial" to require the "Supreme Court" to reverse him?

I would also share with you this opinion taken from a group of lawyers doing business as the Arizona "Supreme Court:"

> "Our Supreme Court has also held the denial of due process is a denial of fundamental fairness, shocking to a universal sense of justice. *Oshrin v. Coulter,* 142 Ariz. 109, 688 P.2d 1001 (1984). See *Kinsella v. U.S. ex rel. Singleton,* 361 US 234, 80 S.Ct. 297, 4 L.Ed.2d 268 (1960)." *State ex rel Romley v. Superior Court,* 172 Ariz. 232.

Apparently violently taking control of the life of another human being isn't "shocking" to these lawyers and their "universal sense of justice." They must be unfamiliar with the following *precedent* so important to lawyers:

> "For, **the very idea that man may be compelled to hold his life, or the means of living, or any material right essential to the enjoyment of life, at the *mere will of another*** seems to be intolerable in any country where freedom prevails, **as being the essence of slavery itself**." *Yick Wo v. Hopkins,* 118 U.S. 356, 370 (emphasis mine).

Evidently, not "intolerable" enough, unless of course, they were silently *exempting* themselves again:

> "By *decisional* law, the rule of necessity overrides the right to life, liberty and property." (Rule 81, Code of Judicial Conduct, commentary for Canon 3E(1)).

It is very telling to compare the *Yick Wo* opinion, above, with both the definition of "statute" from the "Supreme Court" and previous "Senate" opinion:

> "'Statute...The ***written will of the legislature***..." *John P. King Mfg. Co. v. Council of Augusta*, 277 U.S. 100, quoting Bouvier's Law Dictionary (emphasis mine).
>
> "The ultimate ownership of all property is in the State; individual so-called "ownership" is only by virtue of Government, i.e., law, amounting to mere user; and ***that use must be in accordance with law and subordinate to the necessities of the State***." *Senate Resolution* #62, from April 1933 (emphasis mine).

First the "Supreme Court" ruled the "essence of slavery" was to be subject to the "mere will of another..." and then the same group of lawyers is saying a "statute" is the "mere will of another." ***Draw your own conclusions***.

Now getting back to the "plea" being entered *for* me, I would also ask: "if you can enter a plea for me, then can you continue representing me at trial?" It stands to reason, especially if this lawyer sitting four feet off the floor wants to remain *consistent at all*, that if he enters a plea *for* me, then he must also be able to present a defense for me at trial. If he can represent me at the "arraignment," then why not continue doing so at trial? If he says he entered the plea *on my behalf*, then I may also ask, "Can you continue representing me at the trial?" If he then insists the plea was not on my behalf, I would also ask, "if you didn't enter that plea on my behalf, then on whose behalf did you enter it?"

This violent lawyer doesn't have many options left at

this point. This is probably the reason why they are almost always non-responsive. The plea was either entered, one, on my behalf, two, on behalf of the alleged plaintiff or, three, on behalf of the "judge" *himself.* If he did it on behalf of the plaintiff, then, once again, he has a conflict of interest problem and his pretense of fairness is gone. How could a man acting on behalf of the plaintiff enter a plea *for* the *defendant*, and why?

> In his zeal to be fair, impartial, and independent
> he started representing ***both sides***.

If he did it on his own behalf, then he is somehow a party to the case. I would ask him if, in fact, he is a party. This raises the fairness as well as the conflict of interest issue. After all, how can an impartial "judge" enter a plea for me and for himself as well and *at the same time*? Also, how do you enter a "plea" for someone else *on your own behalf*?

This is a rough spot for a "judge" to be in. He has to maintain a pretense of fairness while, at the same time, refusing to accept my plea of guilty and entering a plea *for* me as my lawyer. *And this is while also representing the professed plaintiff.* By this point in time, any perception of fairness is gone and I doubt any rational person is buying into his charade any longer. Instead, the "judge" is starting to strain the patience of all those unfortunately present in "his" courtroom.

I've had a "judge" say I was "refusing to plea" when a proposed plea was on his bench. I had been held on a ransom called a "release bond" and told him I was going to assign the "bond" over to him for the fine. He still *insisted* I was "refusing to plea" and set the matter for a "pre-trial." If I pulled stunts like that I might risk being *institutionalized* and put on medication.

In response to this legal babble, I would object to what the "judge" is doing and leave with a court date in hand, although I might want to consider a change of judge first. The grounds for such a motion would be both the bias and prejudice and conflict of interest already exhibited. Why else would a "judge" refuse to answer a few questions while refusing to accept a plea of responsible or guilty? Also, how does this "judge" explain away the fact *he represents both the plaintiff and myself at the very same time?* In Arizona, if a "judge" does not disqualify himself under such circumstances, I can file a "special action" to have his decisions "reviewed" by a "higher court." This usually stops, at least temporarily, a traffic case. It must, however, be noted that it is just not possible for them to give me a fair trial even if they get another "judge" because each "judge" will still represent the alleged plaintiff. If he does not represent the plaintiff, then he's there on his own. In that case, he's nothing more than an individual violently taking control over my life and cannot, for that reason alone, claim the constitution is his "lawful" "authority."

This lawyer with the robe is a cruel one-man show. He represents both the plaintiff and the defendant while pretending to be independent and impartial. No one else really needs to show up to put on a "trial" because he does it all. It's a no-win situation: if he doesn't represent the plaintiff then he cannot claim to be authorized by the "constitution" without contradicting himself. If he does represent the plaintiff, then the conflict of interest and lack of impartiality is self-evident.

In other words, the "judge" is the ringmaster of a very bad dog and pony show designed to put forth an illusion of justice.

Chapter Nine

What role does the pretended cop play?

One of the "benefits" a traffic case has over a lot of other bureaucratic attacks is the face to face confrontation still available. You are able to confront your accuser in traffic cases unlike situations with the "IRS" where the accuser is protected by an army of attorneys. Once a majority of people start effectively challenging "cops" this confrontation will be denied. This denial will probably be justified with something like this:

> "By decisional law, the rule of necessity may override the rules of cross-examination, evidence and a fair trial." (Rule 81, Code of Judicial Conduct, commentary for Canon 3E(1).

This has already been started. In most areas, the rules of evidence with regards to so-called "civil" cases have been completely wiped out. Arizona, for example, has: "the Arizona Rules of Evidence shall not apply in civil traffic cases" at Rule 19 Arizona Rules of Procedure Civil Traffic Cases. Rule 14 wiped out pre-trial discovery.

If bureaucrats were truly interested in fairness and justice they would have never scrapped their rules of evidence. This is proven by reading what *they* say is the entire purpose for the rules. Keep in mind this was *not* written by a bunch of *bitter non-lawyers* but by "honorable' lawyers:

> "These rules shall be construed to ***secure fairness*** in administration, elimination of unjustifiable expense and delay, and the promotion of growth and development of the law of evidence to ***the end that the truth may be ascertained and proceedings justly determined.***" Rule 102, Arizona Rules of Evidence (emphasis mine).

Well, we bureaucrats can't have "fairness...truth" and "justly determined" proceedings in *traffic* court. If we did that, we'd never win a case, so what do we do? This is what we'll say, "the Arizona Rules of Evidence shall not apply in civil traffic cases." Why else would the rules of evidence be scrapped? Let's see, expediency and costs? No, they say the rules are designed to eliminate "unjustifiable expense and delay." This was done to keep the truth from being "ascertained and [the] proceedings [to be] justly determined."

How many "civil" traffic tickets do you think a "cop" would give out if he were subject to full pre-trial discovery, including depositions, *each and every time*? In that event, a "cop" *could not* give out nearly as many tickets because he would be spending more time submitting to depositions than giving out tickets.

In Arizona, the admitting of evidence is at the sole discretion of the "judge" or "hearing officer." Do you think a man who takes control of another man's life without the latter's consent is going to be fair? No, he's not; especially when he has a financial interest in the outcome of the case. If this politician had any respect for human life and any intention of being fair, then he wouldn't take control of other people's lives by becoming a "judge" or "hearing officer" in the first place. Do you like the idea of violently dominating other people; do you equate that with being fair? And how fair can he be when he represents both the plaintiff and defendant?

There is no merit to any claim the "judge" is "required" by the judicial ethics rules to be "impartial" for no other reason than the fact that:

> "By decisional law, the rule of necessity may override the rule of disqualification." (Rule 81, Code of Judicial Conduct, commentary for Canon 3E(1).

As we have seen throughout this book, the rules mean nothing to these people. It doesn't matter what the rules require when they are ignored, and they can be. Believe it or not, "judges" even have rules saying they can "*suspend*" (ignore) the rules "in the furtherance of justice." This last phrase means to steal property under the guise of "protection."

"Judges" ignore the rules because they'd be out of a job really fast if they didn't.

All of the questions I put to the "judge" at my initial appearance or "arraignment," as they call it, may now also be put to the "cop." After all, this is the individual who made the "complaint" and started this whole mess in the first place. I intend to make him or her support every single legal opinion made against me.

"Cops" usually sign tickets under penalty of perjury or some other kind of pretended certification. What is important here is the ticket contains the "cop's" *testimony*. For example, in Arizona, it says, "I hereby certify upon reasonable grounds, I believe the person named above committed the acts described..." Believe it or not, lawyers have argued with me claiming the ticket is not testimony. Some have claimed that a "revenue agent's" so-called "assessment" was not testimony and neither was the "agent" a witness. Go figure that one out.

This written testimony typically consists of nothing more than a bunch of legal and, or political opinions. This "cop" thinks I "broke the law." He believes I "drove without a license" or some other equally inane legal jargon. This means he has formed at least two legal opinions: he has determined the "law" obligated me in some way to have a "driver's license" and despite this alleged obligation, I failed to have a "license." He has also "certified" he has "reasonable grounds" to support his opinions.

The "cop" signs the ticket either as a "witness," and, in some places, such as Arizona, he signs it as the "complainant" as if he is personally bringing the complaint against you himself. As if not having a seatbelt on is a crime against him personally. However, once the matter is in "court," a little political magic and *sleight of hand* turns the so-called "state" into the alleged complaining party. This is why I say the "state" is just an *alter ego* for the "cop."

At the trial, once the case is called, the "judge" will usually ask if I am ready to proceed. This is only asked to provide the illusion of fairness, the "trial" will go on regardless of my being ready or not. Despite this, I say I'm not because I don't understand the nature and cause of the charges and proceedings against me, therefore, I have a few questions I would like to ask first. This is especially true if there is a lawyer there claiming to be the "state" persecutor. This lawyer, the so-called "prosecutor," does not wear a black robe, though many aspire to (I've noticed many "judges" are former persecutors). He is not supposed to be a witness or a party to the action; maybe it's just me, but I don't remember seeing an attorney standing next to the "cop" during the stop. He is supposed to be *representing* ("to stand in the place of." *Ballentine's Law Dictionary*, page 1095) a party; in this case, the alleged plaintiff (the "state" and, or the "cop" and "judge"). This point is *extremely* important and should not be overlooked.

Try an make sense of this: the "cop" represents the "state" which allegedly includes the "judge," "prosecutor" and me. The "prosecutor" represents the "state" which allegedly includes the "cop," the "judge" and me. The "judge" represents the "state" which allegedly includes the "cop," "prosecutor" and me. Even though not a part of a "state, " the "judge" still represents me when entering a "plea for me. Does this make any sense to you? Still think it's a fair "process?"

I always challenge the "plaintiff's" right to appear in a representative capacity. Though this may really irritate the persecutor and his lawyer wearing the black robe, it's supposed to be a standard "legal challenge." As far as I am aware, every so-called "state" has a rule equivalent to federal rule 9(a) allowing anyone to challenge the appearance of both a lawyer and his alleged client. In Arizona, in "civil" cases, it is called rule 9(a) which states:

> "[W]hen a party desires to raise an issue as to the legal existence of any party or the capacity of any party to sue or be sued or the authority of a party to sue or be sued in a representative capacity, the party desiring to raise the issue shall do so by specific negative averment... "

If you still doubt this is a standard "legal challenge," then have your best friend "represent" you without being a member of a "state bar association" (your local lawyer's union/labor organization/closed shop protection racket). You'll find out real fast just how passionate "judges" and lawyers are about someone being "qualified" to appear in court in a "representative capacity." Keep this in mind if you are not permitted to challenge a lawyer's presence.

I've had a lawyer from a local Arizona "prosecutor's" office tell me, on tape, he could not prove he had a client, and, at the same time, he also thought that *whether he had a client or not was "irrelevant."* Unfortunately, he did not feel the same way about having a "defendant." This lawyer did not believe having a client was *relevant*. Would an honest "judge" permit such nonsense? Would you buy such BS? No less than *five* "honorable" lawyers in Arizona accepted such lunacy.

I filed a "special action" in the Arizona "superior court" against two "city" judges involved in that traffic case. The same "prosecuting" lawyer showed up for the first hearing. I again challenged his appearance under rule 9(a). The "judge" refused to permit it and allowed him to appear *unchallenged* (how's *that* for favoritism?). As he permitted a lawyer to just walk in off the street and appear without a client, this "judge" stated there were no rule 9(a) challenges in "his court." I asked him if special actions were civil cases and he agreed. I then asked him if civil cases were governed by the Arizona Rules of Civil Procedure and he said, "I'm aware of what rules govern these proceedings, what's your point?" I said, "my point is this, if the Arizona Rules of Civil Procedure govern the proceedings, then rule 9(a) applies and I'm going to challenge this lawyer." The "judge" was not pleased and two armed "deputies" suddenly arrived in the courtroom at that point in time in order to "observe." Do "judges" have a ***panic button*** under their bench they can press whenever they feel personally threatened by a rule of court they have sworn to comply with? When all was said and done, no less than four different "judges" permitted this lawyer to appear unchallenged. That indicates a pattern. Apparently, in their mind, it was "necessary" to disregard this rule. After all, a fellow lawyer could not prove he had a client, so to enable him to appear, it was "necessary" to "override" rule 9(a). What a concept-*a lawsuit without a plaintiff.*

On appeal from the traffic court, I again challenged the same lawyer's appearance and the "judge," the fifth one, said this lawyer could appear "unchallenged." OK, I thought, no need to argue. I had Moses with me and told the "judge" I wanted him to assist *me*. The "judge" refused to permit Moses to do so. I said, "...you're permitting [lawyer X] to appear unchallenged, yet you challenge his standing to appear on my behalf? That's not fair."

The "judge" was not happy and "vacated" the hearing saying I should be "shown the door." In other words, as far as this "judge" was concerned it was, "do as I *say*, not as I *do*." Bureaucrats do not like to be one-up'd *at all*.

With bureaucrats it's *always* "My way or the highway."

This "judge" then issued a "minute entry" (a written "order" sent through the "U.S. mail") stating I "refused to address the substantive issues on appeal." So, here he was saying a standard rule 9(a) challenge is a way of refusing to address substantive issues in a traffic case when, in *reality*, it went to the very heart of the case: *there was no complaining party other than some "cop"* who didn't know what a "license," "city," "statute," or a "state" were.

What is "incredible" here is the persecutor *knew* he could not prove he had a client yet it did not stop him and no less than five different "judges" let their fellow lawyer get away with it. ***Why***? Why the consistent pattern of refusing to comply with a basic "rule of court?" What are the odds that this was all an innocent mistake? And why did armed men come into one of the courtrooms? To merely *observe*? And don't forget this is *not an isolated incident*. This happens all the time and regardless of the geographic location. Why the pattern and just as important *how*? And just in case anyone still thinks this is a "frivolous" issue, consider the so-called "law of the land" to wit:

> "[c]ourts must look behind names that symbolize the parties to determine whether a justiciable case or controversy is presented." *United States v. Interstate Commerce Commission*, 337 U.S. 426 at 430 (1949).

Do you see that spewing forth "State of Arizona" *ad nauseam* is not responsive to my question asking if there is *evidence* of a complaining party? The name only *symbolizes* the alleged party. Exactly *what* is being *symbolized* though? Whatever is being symbolized, this lawyer playing "prosecutor" is supposedly "standing in place" of it and his buddies ("judges") will use whatever physical violence is necessary to prevent it from being exposed.

If there *was* evidence of a complaining party then the lawyer acting out as a "prosecutor" could and would have complied with their own sacred "law" and provided it *easily*; after all, "prosecuting" is something they do everyday. However, no less than five "judges" permitted him to appear *unchallenged* and his *own* testimony proved there *was no* complaining party other than the "cop" himself. The only "damage" that might have been caused by my *not* providing this "cop" with ID was that done to his precious ego. How many lawyers would bring a case of "bruised ego" into court? None, unless it's a case for a pretended "state."

> COP: "But, your Honor, I asked for ID and he didn't have any."
>
> JUDGE: "Off with his head!"

Is *death* really too harsh a punishment for not providing ID on demand to some stranger dressed up like a "cop?" Is this really so out of the question? Would a bureaucrat *kill* someone for that? Let's examine that for a moment.

Let's just hypothesize a situation where a man has no ID and, although he is not a threat to anyone as he drives around, a "cop" wants him to stop. This non-violent man chooses not to stop though. In fact, he chooses not to cooperate at all. How is the "cop" going to get this man's car to stop? I need not explain this will involve violence. This violence could lead to the "cop" shooting the man. Even if not murdered on the scene, let's say the man is given a "ticket" and he does not cooperate again by failing to show up in "court." He decided he'd just rather eat cereal and watch cartoons that morning. If a so-called "bench warrant" is then issued, as it will be, "cops" are now "authorized" to use *deadly* force, if necessary, (there's that wonderful word again!), to get him into that building.

I think it's clear to bureaucrats that death is a "just" punishment for not having ID on you. Or maybe death is really just the punishment for bruising the "cop's" ego because his *demands* were not complied with or not complied with *fast enough*. "Your money or your life," or "your ID or your life." What's the difference?

Bureaucrats don't *kill* people for violating

"laws." No, no, no. That's *barbaric*. Bureaucrats only kill people to insure that they stand *trial* for "breaking" those "laws."

Maybe *that* is how bureaucrats get past the "cruel and unusual punishment" clause in the "constitutions."

It was not a "punishment" in the "legal" sense. No, it was the natural consequence of his peaceful disobedience.

Before "proceeding" I ask the lawyer, or the "cop," "is there evidence of a complaining party? Just a simple yes or no answer will do." If the "judge" attempts to interfere on behalf of his cronies, I ask the "judge," "who has the burden of proof here?" "Judges" in traffic courts usually need to be *reminded* it is supposedly the plaintiff, and not the defendant (us, their victims) that has the burden of proof. If so, I might point out the following rule:

> "The judge presiding at the trial may not testify in that trial as a witness. No objection need be made in order to preserve the point." Rule 605, Arizona Rules of Evidence.

Perhaps this is the reason why the rules of evidence were thrown out in "civil traffic cases." Maybe by doing so it "permits" the "judge" to testify against me without submitting to cross-examination. The burden of proof is *supposed* to be on the complaining party "beyond a reasonable doubt" in "criminal cases" and "by a preponderance of the evidence" in "civil cases." The "judge," *consistent with the rules, common sense and fairness*, is not permitted to jump in and answer such questions for the plaintiff. *This is true even if he does represent the plaintiff.* Marcia Clark was not permitted to testify for Kato for goodness sakes. Again, I would ask the "judge" what is his role in this if he insists on helping (representing) the alleged plaintiff. ***If he insists on having the "right" to repeatedly jump in and testify then I will remind him of my "right" to cross-examine him.*** I will also remind him of rule 605.

As previously shown, evidence of a complaining party does not consist of merely having the *name* of that party such as "the state." If that's all they can or will provide, I will tell them that such an answer is non-responsive to a question which only requires a yes or no answer. What in the world is so *difficult* about answering yes or no???

I don't let the "cop," "judge," or lawyer get off point here. This point is *critical* in that it does more to expose them than almost anything else I can think of at this point in my experience. That's why I keep asking them even if they tend to get very upset. It is easier to see why this is so important if you look at it this way: imagine you get served with a summons and complaint from people you have never heard of before. Do you just accept they have standing to complain?

Think about this for a moment, why would politicians get upset just because I am asking for *evidence* of a complaining party? The reason is because, like the lawyer who said who he was representing was "irrelevant," they *know* they cannot provide any facts to prove there is a complaining party other than *themselves.* But *who* are *they*? Who are these violent strangers presuming to have the "right" to interfere with my life and that of others without anyone's freely given consent?

Bureaucrats act on behalf of themselves under a collective alter ego known as "the state;" a thinly concealed protection racket.

I am exposing the fact that the phrase the "State of Arizona," or "City of San Diego" etc., is just an *alter ego* shared by the "cop," the "prosecutor" and the lawyer representing them both, the pretended "judge." It is merely an *idea,* a "mental conception" or fantasy that has no real, tangible existence outside of someone's head. It's just like Santa Claus; yes, people can dress up as Santa Claus, but that doesn't make them Santa Claus. "Santa Claus" is just an idea that may have once seemed very real to you but, as you grew up, it no longer did, and for good reason. **There is no "state"** and that's why "judges" refuse to comply with rule 9(a) and such precedent from the "Supreme Court" quoted above: "courts must look behind names that symbolize the parties..."

The difference, however, between Santa Claus and the "state" is that no one is using a gun to force me to believe in Santa and, if someone did, they wouldn't be hailed as a "hero" or "honorable."

Other than their guns and an insatiable appetite for violence and domination, the only thing bureaucrats have are their opinions. For example, I once had a "judge" in Arizona tell me the "State of Arizona" was an "act of congress from 1911." Who was I to argue with her (other than pointing out she was *testifying* against me on behalf of the "cop")? How is an "act of congress" a complaining party? What *obligation* do I owe, and how did I *damage* an alleged "act of congress?" Better yet, exactly *where, when, why* and *how* was I "within" or "subject to" an "act of congress?"

By her own admission the "State of Arizona" was not the ground. That, however, was the "cop's" *only* basis to claim that I was "within the state." Do you think the "cop" was thinking of "an act of congress" when he testified I was "within the state?"

> "Yeah, this is officer Gruden; I'm observing a white male within an act of congress *without* ID, send back-up NOW! *Lot's of back-up.*"

Even if I were to accept the opinion that the "state" had a tangible existence such as a group of men and women, why should I accept the opinion this "cop" or some lawyer, *represents* every one of them? How about their opinion that there was a cause of action against me? How did I damage this group of people? What possible *obligations* could I have to this group of unidentified people and why? You see? This is why I question *everything*. The more you examine what these people say and do, the more it falls apart.

The "state" is not a *natural* phenomenon. It is *man-made* and *exists only in the mind.* There are no naturally created "states." They are *all* artificial. Prior to July 4th, 1776, there were no American "states," there were allegedly American "*colonies*." The "colonies" were magically transformed into "states" by nothing more than words being scribbled onto pieces of paper called "constitutions." However, unless you believe in childish ideas such as magic, then you know that words on paper create nothing.

Currently (summer 2002), there is a lot of talk about a Palestinian "state" in the Middle East. The land is there and the Palestinians are there, but where is their so-called "state?"

> **A "state" is nothing more than a "state" of mind. A "nation" is nothing more than a halluci-Nation. A "country" is ... starting to get the picture?**

You see, merely by *asking*, "is there *evidence* of a complaining party?" I am exposing the fact ***there isn't one***, at least, not a *tangible* one. *There's just an illusion in someone's head.* In other words:

There is no "state."

As I like to put it: can I hit a "state" with a rock? To put the question differently, can I put a "government" in a wheelbarrow? No, I can't. In stark terms, we can destroy the physical infrastructure of a "country" but, if the people remain, the "state" remains because their "country" (group identity) was all in their heads to begin with, not their *land*. They merely associate their "country" with "their" land.

Many think the "state" *is* the *ground*, that the geographic landmass "Arizona" is identical in all respects to the "*State of* Arizona." This is not only false, this is absurd, and for many reasons. I will provide only one more example. If the "state" were the ground and ONLY the ground (*just as a table is just a table and not a book on the table*), then the complaining party in a traffic case would be *the ground*. Now *that's* insane.

Obviously the "state" is not the ground. A "state" is not geographic or even tangible; if it's anything, then it's *political*. The shocking reality behind all of this is if evidence could be admitted to prove there is a group of individuals out there who entered into some sort of agreement, there is still no evidence I'm obligated to them or have damaged them in any way.

To think I can somehow damage someone in Page Arizona if I don't have ID on me when driving down the street in Phoenix to get a box of raisins (or other dry fruit) is "patently" *insane*. Anyone with such a belief would be laughed at as a nutcase. However, put a costume on that same individual, give him a gun, a really cool looking badge, a car with fancy lights on top, and total lack of discretion and personal responsibility and…

That is why I may also ask, "is there evidence of a cause of action against me?" I keep a record of their answers as best I can because the odds are they are going to be non-responsive to each and every question. I also like to point out the contradictions whenever they arise. Being non-responsive is itself proof the so-called "trial" is unfair. As previously stated, the "Supreme Court" holds the opinion that to satisfy "due process," a hearing must be "meaningful." It hardly needs demonstrating that being non-responsive falls far short of being truly "meaningful."

And, on that point, can a "trial" based on violence be "meaningful" to begin with? To then add almost complete non-responsiveness to the violence certainly seems extreme and unnecessary, unless, of course, the "Supreme Court" believes "meaningful" means "sham," "charade," "joke" etc.

Not surprisingly, the "judge" will usually ignore my questions and pretend I'm not even there. They do this by calling the "cop" up to the witness stand to testify despite any and all objections I may raise. If you see this in person you'll know, first hand, that these proceedings have nothing to do with fairness. I have had "cops" admit in depositions they lacked personal knowledge of the facts and "judges" have still permitted them to testify. Indeed, these "trials" resemble a "dog and pony" show, and a *bad one at that.* I mean, some of these so-called "judges" don't even give you pretense of fairness, that's how ridiculous they are. No, to them, naked aggression is the rule.

That is why I am *never* permitted to videotape the proceedings and there is never a reason given despite the fact the rules permit it (even so, in "Legal Land" "judges" don't have to give reasons for anything). It boggles the imagination when you consider that, in the "Mesa City Court," so-called "criminal" proceedings are videotaped *everyday*. Just walk in and you can see several being *broadcast in the lobby.*

During direct examination, if the persecutor or the "judge" asks the "cop" a question that "assumes facts not in evidence," I object on those grounds. This is basically his *entire* testimony though. There is humor somewhere in there, but I'm not laughing.

Most of the "cop's" testimony will consist of rambling "time worn" legal opinions such as his seeing me within a pretended "city." Well, unless a "city" is a particular geographic area and *nothing* else (it's not), then our "cop" has assumed facts not in evidence. He has also drawn a legal opinion that is supposed to be based upon facts already in evidence. The "judge" will really expose his true nature if he overrules this objection. It is unfair to permit a witness to assume facts not in evidence. Just ask any lawyer.

A big one is if the lawyer asks the "cop" a question requiring him to draw a legal opinion or conclusion, such as "did you see Marc commit a crime" or "driving without a license?" This is a very serious glitch in the "system" I've exploited for years. They will *always* allow the "cop" to testify he saw me commit a "crime" or violate a so-called "statute." However, if I ask questions any more difficult or probing than that, the lawyer and the "judge" will run to the rescue of their client (partner) and refuse to allow him to answer any such questions. That's exactly the point of the questions though; to make them run full bore into a corner.

If I object to a question requiring the "cop" to offer an opinion such as "I saw Marc violate a statute," and the "judge" *overrules* that objection, I don't worry because I know the "judge" will contradict himself later on when it's my turn to "cross-examine" the "cop."

The "judge" is headed for a pretty bad time for allowing the "cop" to continue giving legal opinions because he has permitted the "cop" to assume facts not in evidence and has overruled my objection that a question called for a legal conclusion.

My "cross-examination" is geared to taking advantage of these "rulings" by helping the "judge" back himself into a corner so he will contradict himself and throw out every rule of fairness in his sacred little "law" books. I know from experience that "cops" will not be permitted to answer questions such as "what is a statute?" That is why I deliberately set them up to contradict themselves. Some lawyers have proudly proclaimed the "cop" doesn't need to know what a "statute" is to prove I "violated" one. *Really*? **Maybe you can also perform brain surgery without knowing the brain is in the skull**. Where is the "personal knowledge?" Without the lawyerese, shouldn't the bare minimum for a witness to be credible be that he at least knows what he's talking about?

The point is not to be argumentative, but to get the case thrown out so I can go back to being productive instead of *wasting* my time with these crooks dressed in suits, robes, and other idiotic uniforms.

Chapter Ten

How I cross-examine a bureaucrat

My objective in questioning bureaucrats (whether a pretended "cop," "revenue agent," or any other imposter, charlatan, swindler etc.) is to show there is no case against me, *except groundless legal opinions backed by violence.* The only effective way I know of doing this is to ask him what facts his "legal" opinions are based on. This essentially strips bare all of the deletions, distortions and additions to reality the "cop" (or other bureaucrat) has made. Remember the example with the salesman earlier? If a salesman throws you a line of BS about his product, then the easiest way to prove he's a con man is to ask him to demonstrate it. You just sit back and watch the moron embarrass himself.

According to their *own* bureaucratic rules and "precedent," I'm *supposed* to be able to question the "cop" on *all* his prior testimony and any "new" testimony the "judge" relies on. This includes challenging any documentary and, or other evidence being used against me. Refusal to permit this is *supposed* to be one of the worst errors "judges" can make:

> "***Undue restrictions on the right to cross-examine strikes at the very heart of the adversary system***: "*** '[a] ***denial of cross-examination*** without waiver *** would be a constitutional ***error of the first magnitude and no amount of showing of want of prejudice would cure it.'*** *Brookhart v. Janis,* 384 US 1, 3, 86 S.Ct 1245, 1246, 16 L.Ed.2d 314." *Smith v. Illinois,* 390 US 129, 131, 88 S.Ct. 748, 750, 19 L.Ed.2d 956, 959 (1968)." *State v. Hanley,* 108 Ariz. 144, 148, 493 P.2d 1201 (emphasis added).

Before any lawyers protest, "this is *only* for so-called criminal cases," please reference the following precedent:

> "***This Court has been zealous to protect these*** [confrontation] ***rights from erosion. It has spoken out not not only in criminal cases,*** e. g., Mattox v. United States, 156 U.S. 237, 242-244; Kirby v. United States, 174 U.S. 47; Motes v. United States, 178 U.S. 458, 474; In re Oliver, 333 U.S. 257, 273, ***but also in all types of cases where administrative and regulatory actions were under scrutiny***. e.g., Southern R. Co. v. Virginia, 290 U.S. 190; Ohio Bell Telephone Co. v. Public Utilities Commission, 301 U.S. 292; Morgan v. United States, 304 U.S. 1, 19; Carter v. Kubler, 320 U.S. 243; Reilly v. Pinkus, 338 U.S. 269." *Green v. McElroy*, 360 U.S. 474, 496-497 (1959) (emphasis mine).

This "Supreme Court" then quoted the following in regards to confrontation:

> "For two centuries past, the policy of the Anglo-American system of Evidence has been to regard ***the necessity of testing by cross-examination as a vital feature of the law***. The belief that no safeguard for testing the value of human statements is comparable to that furnished by ***cross-examination***, and the conviction that ***no statement*** (unless by special exception) ***should be used as testimony until it has been probed and sublimated by that test, has found increasing strength in lengthening experience***." (Emphasis mine)

Even without these opinions, it's common sense and

self-evident that using evidence not subject to challenge is unfair and a mockery of "justice," if there is such a thing in these lawyer made and lawyer run "courts." The whole point of a trial is to give you an opportunity to defend yourself; to essentially *test* the "evidence" being used against you. As previously stated, ***calling it a "trial" is itself a lie.*** Even the lawyers pretending to be a "Supreme Court" agree: "By agreeing to this truncated kind of trial - if trial it could be called..." *Brookhart v. Janis*, 384 U.S. 1, at 6. If one cannot challenge the pretended "evidence," then what's the point and why require my presence at the barrel of a gun? Public relations; classic diversion.

I *want* the lawyer *and* the "judge" to say the "cop" *cannot* testify because my "question calls for a legal conclusion." That is my opportunity to ask the "judge" if the "cop's" entire testimony, including the ticket, should be stricken from the record. In other words, treated as though it never existed and the complaint was never made. I also want to point out the "judge's" previous "ruling" where he did allow the "cop's" legal opinions to become a permanent part of the record. Always expect contradictions.

This is accomplished by *purposely* asking the "cop" if he witnessed me commit a "crime" or a "civil" violation (I can ask the same question the "prosecutor" asked earlier). Which is, of course, what started this mess in the first place. Chances are, there will be no objection to this question and that is *precisely* what I want, just one more inconsistency. The "cop" will say yes, and I might even show him his ticket in order to help him out, assuming he needs the help.

I then ask, "was that an arbitrary opinion?" If he understands what arbitrary means (believe it or not, some "cops" don't), then he will answer, "no." I then ask, "so that opinion was based upon facts currently within your knowledge?" He will probably answer, "yes."

This is not an enviable position to be in as a witness. *He's just testified that he has facts to support his opinion the "law" was obligatory on me.* However, his entire testimony consists of nothing but inane legal opinions he learned in the police academy and the police department locker room.

I have questioned "IRS" agents in the same way and have been quickly shown the door. In some cases men and women D/B/A the "IRS" have refused to permit hearings and settlement conferences because they just can't support their barrage of legal gibberish. If they do not, or cannot, tell me the facts, then both their pretended "case" and pretense of good faith are gone. They are either concealing evidence or they lied about having it in the first place. Refusing to answer questions is also grounds to get testimony stricken. That is why there is no need to fight or argue. I had a supervisor at the "Arizona Department of Revenue" tell me his subordinate "had every right not to answer questions" in regards to a "subpoena" he served on someone. I then reminded them that I didn't care whether the question was answered or not because the "judge" then had every right to quash his beloved "subpoena." So go right ahead and refuse to answer questions.

I then ask the "cop," "what are those facts?" This usually causes the persecutor to immediately stand up objecting on the grounds the "witness may not testify because it calls for a legal conclusion;" the same objection I previously made. The "judge" then obediently sustains the objection oblivious to the fact I asked for the *facts* and not another nonsensical "legal" opinion. At this point, I don't argue with them or say they are wrong other than to point out I only asked for the *facts*, the legal conclusion had *already* been drawn again without objection.

The "judge" (as well as the other two bureaucrats in the courtroom) is now in a particularly difficult spot. He may have previously *overruled* my objection the witness (the "cop") could not draw legal conclusions and has already permitted the "cop" to testify that he witnessed me commit a "crime" or "civil" violation which is, itself, a "legal" conclusion. *He has now sustained the exact same objection with the same witness.* The judge's actions are now plainly inconsistent and to my obvious prejudice; so much so that even a non-lawyer can tell it isn't fair.

To make the "judge" even more uncomfortable, I then ask, "O.K., since the witness may not draw legal opinions, then shouldn't his testimony, including the ticket, be stricken from the record?" This is a checkmate for the "judge." If he refuses to strike the testimony and ticket, then he may not deny cross-examination. If so, this is supposed to be a huge "incurable" error on the part of the "judge" and should be reversed on appeal.

I would then ask, "are you going to rely on the witness's testimony?" He may not answer this question, but his actions will establish whether he is or he is not.

If he does strike the testimony, then the case is over because, without any testimony there is no evidence and without any evidence, there is no case. Without a case, the "judge" would be basing his "decision" entirely upon his own opinion. Despite happening every day in traffic courts, this is unfair because the "judge" is witnessing against me and I cannot cross-examine the "judge." *Unless he wants to jump in the witness chair he shouldn't be pretending to be a witness.* Indeed, the "judge" has nothing whatsoever to do with the case except for the fact that he is now trying to profit off of it. The same holds true for any lawyer who claims to be representing the pretended plaintiff, the intangible so-called "state."

I also point out that the "judge" previously *overruled* the same objection that a question called for a legal conclusion on the part of the "cop" and now he is *sustaining* the exact same objection. Excuse me Mr. "honorable" lawyer, but which one is it?

If you don't believe any of this try it for yourself during your next encounter with a "judge." Watch how the "judge" toys with you as though he's a great big cat and you're just a little old mouse or a ball of string. For the time being, believe it or not:

The same witness *can* and *cannot* answer ques-

tions that call for a "legal" conclusion.

This is classic "Legal Land" nonsense where the very same objection, with the very same witness, gets a "yes" from the same "judge" in one instance and a "no" from the same "judge" in another, and all in the same case! Does this remind you of "Alice in Wonderland?" This sort of "now you see it, now you don't" "legal" trickery is commonplace in American courtrooms. In fact, this reminds me of a line from that classic tale by Lewis Carroll:

> "Nothing would be what it is, because everything would be what it isn't. And contrary-wise -what it is, it wouldn't be. And what it wouldn't be, it would. You see?" That's how bureaucrats *really* talk!

Can you imagine if your *doctor* did *his* job with this same degree of *precision*? "You need heart surgery...then again you don't;" "you're going to die in six months...well there's really nothing wrong with you." How about a plumber, how long he would be in business if he acted like these "judges?"

> **That pipe's busted pretty bad and, well, it's just not. It is and, well, it isn't.**

A plumber couldn't get away with such lunacy because he can't hold his customers in "contempt."

Imagine going to a store and you go to the check out counter with a box of raisins marked $2.99. The cashier tells you the raisins are $150.00 plus administrative costs for his having to ring you up. You tell him the raisins are marked $2.99 and that's all you're going to pay for them, and only an imbecile would pay $150.00 for a little box of raisins.

The cashier gets angry and says, "It's *my* register, you're in *my* line, it's *my* store and you are going to pay $150!"

You tell him that's not how you understand it; the box is clearly marked $2.99. He says that's "your interpretation," it costs what *he* says it costs and if you don't like it, hire another grocer to explain it to you. You refuse, give the raisins back and start leaving so you can buy raisins from a *normal* person.

The cashier then snaps at you that you're now in ***contempt of store*** and you have to pay not only the $150 to be released from the store, but you also must pay the costs of "keeping you there." If you don't like it, you can "appeal" it to the store's manager *after* you've paid this new bill.

If you somehow manage to get away from this nutcase, he might then "issue a warrant" and give it to store "security" who would then be "authorized" to use deadly force to "arrest" you and bring you back to "his store." And if that's not bad enough, the cashier has no personal liability for his actions because cashiers must be free and independent.

Would anyone accept such behavior from a cashier? If not, then why do they accept it from a pack of lawyers? What separates cashiers from lawyers; why are lawyers able to foist this madness on others while cashiers can not? Cashiers do not provide their services at the barrel of a gun.

Getting back to my cross-examination of the "cop." Other questions I may ask have to do with the other legal opinions the "cop" has already made. Good examples are I was "driving without a license" and that I am "within a city" or a "state."

It's always a good idea to ask the "cop" to *repeat* his prior testimony, for example, "is it your testimony that I was driving without a license?" This question tends to upset "judges" and "persecutors." Another is, "Is it your testimony I was driving while my privilege to do so was suspended?" Why get upset? All I am doing is having the "cop" repeat his prior testimony. After all, he has already claimed it on the ticket and I am supposed to have the "right" to confront all witnesses against me. However, "judges" appear to know the "cop" cannot provide any facts the opinion was based because *there are no facts.* A great question is to explain what a "privilege" is *factually* and do so without using the word "license." The "judge" and the "cop's" other lawyer will not permit the "cop" to even attempt the answer such a question.

I was once in the Phoenix "superior court" on a new trial for a traffic ticket. A client had impeached the "cop" in the "trial" in the Scottsdale "justice court" and yet the "judge" said the "cop's" testimony was "irrelevant." How's that for a big surprise? *This "judge" was actually saying a man was guilty of a "crime" while the "judge" himself was admitting there was no evidence*! Not surprisingly, after this case was lost and appealed, the "judge" just happened to "lose" the *entire* record of the case. That is why the "superior court" had to order a "new trial."

The charge was driving on a "suspended license," *whatever* that's supposed to mean. All my client did was ask the "cop" sitting on the witness stand if that was his testimony. The persecutor pretending to represent the "state" jumped to his feet objecting on the grounds that answering this question called for a legal conclusion. Apparently this lawyer failed to recognize this legal conclusion was *already* on the ticket he so desperately relied on for a ostensible conviction. Just feed their opinions back in the form of a question.

The "judge" refused to permit the "cop" to answer the question. The client asked why the "cop" could not verify his own prior testimony and the "judge" got *furious* and started yelling. I stood up and said this was only the charge on the ticket in question, so what was the big deal? Per the "judge's" order I was then escorted out of the courtroom by two armed men called "deputies."

The "deputies" were stunned at what the "judge" had done. *They asked me to explain what just happened.* They could not understand why the "judge" refused to permit the "cop" to answer what the charge was. Those two "deputies" were ready to use whatever violence was necessary to get me out of that courtroom and yet they had no idea *why.* "We was just following orders."

The reason why the "judge" did not want the "cop" to verify his own prior written testimony presented on his own traffic ticket, or to even discuss it, was simple:

It was an arbitrary "legal" opinion.

It was pure fantasy and those two lawyers knew it. I testified at this "trial" as an expert witness in Arizona criminal and traffic law *without* challenge. The "judge" was not happy at all about this. Based on my testimony the "cop" was "thoroughly impeached" as a witness. The "cop's" legal opinion was *supposed* to have been stricken and not considered by the "judge." The only way it can be considered, consistent with fairness and with the rules of court (when they are actually being applied), is to permit cross-examination of the witness. This was not permitted which, in and of itself, proves there was no case. It's one or the other.

By using this approach the "judge" puts *himself* in a serious bind and has to choose between either exposing the true nature of the "trial," that being the taking of property by means of physical violence and nothing more, or maintaining a pretense of fairness. Remember, this is a *pretense* of fairness; nothing based on violence is fair.

In my experience, one of these two will always be "sacrificed" in these situations. Which one depends on who the "judge" is on that particular day. If he sacrifices the perception of fairness and chooses physical violence, or threats of violence, then nothing will change his mind, not even having the "cop" testify on my behalf, which has happened before. The principal at work in such a case is:

> "**contra negantem principia non est disputandum**...It is useless to dispute with one who denies principals." *Ballentine's Law Dictionary*, page 265.

Such a person cannot, and should not be reasoned with because they only understand physical violence. In other words, unless a "judge" higher up on the political pecking order tells him he's wrong, he is not going to listen to me. He will not even listen to his *own* "witness," so obviously, I can't sway him either.

In my experience, more often than not, "judges" choose to sacrifice their pretense of fairness, even if they ultimately throw a case out. This isn't the worst thing that can happen though because the subsequent appeal can be quite embarrassing for the "state" attorney trying to defend this "judge's" actions. He wants to maintain a pretense of fairness just as well. This is why I said by making tangible evidence the central issue I am able to *sanitize* a case by removing most of the prejudicial elements against me. This is what I want if I have to "appeal."

On appeal, I have one critical issue: the "judge" accepted the "cop's" testimony without challenge. He ruled the witness could testify, then could *not* testify and refused to permit me to cross-examine him. He then relied on that same unchallenged testimony which consisted of nothing more than arbitrary and incomprehensible legal jargon.

You don't have to go to "law school" to see that it's unfair to accept testimony from a witness not competent to testify. If I cannot win on this issue, and this issue alone, then anything else probably doesn't stand a chance because so-called "appellate courts" are also a joke. This is why my last appeal memorandum was only a page and a half long.

On appeal, the lawyer for the pretended "state" has to somehow justify what the "judge" has done. Now put yourself in his shoes. What in the world would you say to justify these contradictory acts on the part of the "judge?" How do you justify the taking of unchallenged legal opinions? Do you see now why the word judge, cop and trial are always in quotes?

I can't think of any justification for all of this and that

is probably why, in all except one traffic case, the lawyer for the "state" did not even bother to file a reply brief. In the one recent case where a lawyer from Arizona *did* file a reply memorandum, he lied by intentionally deleting part of reality. He claimed I never asked the witness about the facts even though at least seven witnesses would disagree. In fact, this lawyer also *disagreed* when I questioned him *outside* a courtroom; he admitted I had asked the "cop" about the facts. This and other cases taught me that in "Legal Land" the facts and truth are "irrelevant." This also helped to reinforce my belief there is no way out of a situation like this *except* for the bureaucrat to lie or just be non-responsive. That's when I know I caught them with their pants down; they either fall silent or start spewing forth verbal diarrhea.

Another example is a tax case I helped someone out with in California. There was an administrative hearing before four individuals doing business as the "Board of Equalization" and the subject was a so-called "tax assessment."

I made an application for subpoenas so the alleged "witnesses" would appear at the hearing for cross-examination. The application was denied, not once, but *three* times, on the grounds the witnesses "lacked personal knowledge of the facts." The first two times this decision was made by "staff lawyers" so any claims the decision was "legally defective" and a "nullity," are "without merit and frivolous," according to their own rhetoric, not mine. So what did I do? I didn't argue. *I agreed*:

> **There can be *no* personal knowledge of facts that *don't* exist.**

In their enthusiasm to steal property these politicians impeached the very witnesses they relied on. I pointed out that section 702 of the California evidence code made the testimony "inadmissible" and I asked for that testimony, which consisted of this so-called "tax assessment" to be stricken (thrown out). In classic bureaucratic style, these four individuals refused. *Keeping in mind the opinion the witnesses lacked personal knowledge was theirs and not mine*:

> **Why would four allegedly "neutral" individuals all accept opinions they knew were arbitrary?**

Consider the disregard these four men and women had for the *divine* "law" they are allegedly sworn to "preserve, protect, and defend..." These bureaucrats were so eager to rob this man they ignored their very own "rulings."

Once in court their lawyer wanted the *videotape* of that tragic comedy (pretended hearing) thrown out and stricken from the record. Why? Because, it proves this lawyer had no admissible evidence to base her *opinions* on and no amount gyrating and screaming about "taxes," "liabilities," "laws" and whatever else was relevant because she was not a party or a witness.

Think of it this way: Imagine if O.J. Simpson were put on trial with no more "evidence" than the mere *opinions* of Marcia Clark and her fellow lawyers pretending to represent a "state." There is no Kato and no forensics. In fact, there is absolutely nothing but the opinions of some lawyers who profit from such "proceedings." No rational adult would accept this as fair and yet this is standard and happens *every single day* in traffic and tax cases (among other bureaucratic attacks). Where are all the public demonstrations? Where is the ACLU?

To clarify even further I will give you several examples of mere legal opinions that somehow pass as tangible "evidence" in traffic courts and other parts of "Legal Land"

> I am "within the state."
> I am "within the city."
> I am "a resident of the state."
> I am "subject to the jurisdiction of ..."
> I "violated a law."

> I "violated a statute."
> I "must appear in court."
> This or that other "statute applies."

Just the words "state" and "city" represent nothing tangible and are only political jargon. In lay terms, *they are in and of themselves lies.* In regards to traffic cases, these would be the legal opinions of a "cop." They are opinions, not facts. *They do not qualify as facts any more than my opinions qualify as facts.* Think about this because it's important, *very important.* The words "state" and "city" represent or *symbolize* nothing more than *abstractions* with no *tangible* existence outside of the "cop's" mind, and the minds of his victims; you, for example. And keep in mind that what a "cop" purports to do in place of a licensed attorney is *supposed to* be a "nullity."

In the above "tax" case, the witnesses claimed the person I was helping was "within the state." By the Board of Equalization's *own admission,* the witnesses "lacked personal knowledge of the facts." Are you starting to see just how similar Alice's "Wonderland" and "Legal Land" really are? If so, is it *possible* that what you think is "real" is just a public relations scheme? Are your perceptions and reality one and the same? What if your life is nothing more than a lie rammed down your throat since you were a child?

> If the ground were the "state" and the man I was helping admitted to being *physically* located in California, then ***why*** would these politicians claim the witnesses "lacked personal knowledge of the facts?"

These bureaucrats accuse people of being "within the state" everyday to justify their violence and yet they are not permitted to testify to the same under oath? *What does this tell you about both the people who parade around as a "government" and the true nature of the so-called "state?"*

There is no "state"

Despite being *physically* in California these bureaucrats could not testify the man was "within the state" because in *their* opinion they "lacked personal knowledge of the facts." They not only impeached the witnesses *themselves*, denied cross-examination, and accepted arbitrary opinions as tangible evidence, but they *sanctioned* the man I was helping the maximum allowed by their so-called "law." These four politicians claimed both the man's position was "patently frivolous" and sanctions of five thousand dollars were warranted. His position? His position was the opinions against him were not supported by facts. *This is the same position two staff lawyers and the four bureaucrats themselves held.* Only in "Legal Land" can the exact same position be both "frivolous" and NOT "frivolous" at the very same time.

Another example of the political dream world is the word "law" itself. This word is *hypnotic.* Most people give it no thought at all and accept it blindly. Some people, like "cops," are willing to *murder* in its name. Indeed, no act is too vicious if it's the "law."

To help you understand a "law" is just an opinion backed by violence, think about the process that leads to a pretended "law's" creation, *from a lay standpoint of course.* In other words, let's look at the facts, and nothing more, without any political spin or rhetoric.

Some man or woman prancing around as a pretended "legislator" says to other men and women pretending to be "legislators" that, in his/her *opinion*, everyone *must* have a "driver's license." They count noses and if a majority holds the same *opinion*, then that *opinion* is re-named a "law." There is still nothing *tangible* though and it doesn't matter if that opinion is then written up in fancy "law" books because you could easily burn those books. Would that be the end of that particular "law?" After being re-named the "law" this mere collective *opinion* is then forced upon other people by armed troops more commonly known as "cops." Think about this for a moment:

> **What if the "law" was not *written down* and all the bureaucrats put their guns down? Would this change how easily it was accepted?**

In addition to that, what if the "cop" didn't have his costume (uniform) and neat looking badge on? Let's say he was wearing a t-shirt, sneakers and reeked of beer. Does this change your perception that he is an alleged "authority?"

Because I know from experience some people will have a problem with the above example and throw up the "murder" argument, I will provide the following. Some people may think we need "laws" for things like murder and rape. This however, neglects reality because I am unaware of "laws" *prohibiting* murder and other real crimes to wit:

> "**13-1102. Negligent homicide; classification**
> A. A person commits negligent homicide if with criminal negligence such person causes the death of another person.
> B. Negligent homicide is a class 4 felony."
> Arizona Revised Statutes.

Notice this is only a "classification" and prescribed level of punishment. This appears to be consistent, *see* also 76-5-201 Utah, 782.04 of Florida as well as others. There is no attempt by a gang of faceless, unproductive men and women (politicians, bureaucrats) to criminalize the above act because it would be redundant.

I want to make one last point in regards to the "law" and its hypnotic power on people because I think this power is lost when it is seen for what it really is. Let's say the men and women who parade around as "congressmen" pass a "law" there would be no more *gravity*: the legislature finds that without gravity the costs of shipping would be reduced thereby helping the economy of the state. Would you happily waltz off the top of the Sears Tower? If not, *then why*?

What if they passed a "law" that rocks were now apples? Would you take a big bite of a block of granite? Shouldn't we respect and comply with *all* "laws," at least until they are declared "unconstitutional" by the courts or "repealed" by the "legislature?"

Before you think these are absurd examples, consider the fact that a "legislature" in the south, I believe it was Alabama, passed a "law" forbidding a river from rising past a certain level. When you just look at the facts, the "law" starts to lose its hypnotic dream like power.

What is important here is a group of men and women are forcing other men and women to accept, or *at least act on*, their "mental conception." *What* the "mental conception" is, is *irrelevant* and beside the point. The important thing here is the coercion and violence used to get people to accept or at least act on "mental conceptions."

To use another example: The alphabet is invaluable to communication and needs no explanation to show why it is valuable to learn it. Now, just imagine using violence to teach the alphabet to children. In that instance, the children would not actually *learn* anything. Instead, they would be *conditioned* to respond in a certain way to avoid violence. That is how some *animals* are trained. Choice is taken away and replaced with fear of violence.

In my experience there is a common misconception that a "city" or "state" is a natural phenomenon like an ocean, a mountain or another part of the earth. As previously discussed, many think it's a geographic area or land mass such as a continent or island. *According to lawyers with and without black robes, nothing could be further from the truth.* I say that because *in their own words* a "state" is *not* a geographic area. There is Arizona and then there is the "State of Arizona." As stated earlier, if the "state" was the ground and *only* the ground, then the lawyer playing "prosecutor" represents the ground. Am I the only one who thinks such a premise is crazy?

Fairness requires consistency. The "cop" has an opinion that I am "within the state," subject to his "jurisdiction" and I "broke the law." These are just opinions or labels and not a statement of facts. The cruelest labels I'm aware of are the words "legal" and "lawful." The following is critical to remember:

> **The words "legal" and "lawful" have no real *meaning*, only a *purpose*.**

That purpose is to justify some of the most heinous acts you can think of by men and women pretending to be a "state," sort of *linguistic subterfuge*. Any moral or ethical conviction a man may have is thrown out the window if an act is deemed "legal." A good example is slavery. The opposite is also true. Just as people who currently take or sell certain drugs are seen as criminals against whom the "government" "must" wage a "war"on, if the drug "laws" were "repealed" tomorrow those very same people would be *instantly* converted to honest "law-abiding citizens." There are people who sell drugs everyday of the week and instead of being considered criminals they are called *doctors* and *pharmacists*. Why no war on doctors and pharmacists?

The phrase "war on drugs" itself is a lie *because it's not a war on drugs*; it's a war against the people who sell or use them without a "state license."

I don't use drugs and I do not advocate their use. However, being a non-violent and peaceful man, I choose not to force my personal beliefs on others. I have to laugh when I drive down the street and see signs such as: "drug-free school zone." If that were true, the teachers wouldn't be taking Prozac and none of the children taking Ritalin, both are mood-altering drugs.

Someone please tell me what the "*substantive*" difference

is between taking mood-altering drugs such as Prozac and "recreational" drugs besides the political mantra "one is legal, the other is not." What's the difference between a teacher who uses cocaine as opposed to a teacher who uses Prozac? Drink a six-pack in your living room while smoking cigarettes and watching a baseball game and you're an all-American guy and good "citizen." However, smoke a joint while watching the same game one house over from the beer-chugging smoker and you're a "felon" who belongs in prison.

Only in "Legal Land" is such nonsense taken seriously. If you accept the premise another person has the right to control what you ingest, such as heroin, then you must accept the premise that another person has the right to force you to eat only certain kinds of foods. If your neighbor has no right to force you not to eat pork rinds, then guess what? That's right, if your neighbor doesn't have such right, then the men and women valiantly "representing" him don't either. Could you imagine a "war on pork rinds?" Sixty machine gun toting "pork rind warriors" raided an underground convenience store... The only important issue with drugs is that another person is using violence to control what you ingest. For goodness sake, it's very easy for little children to choke on bread and pizza crust, should there be a "war on bread" also?

It's not a matter of what you are forced to ingest or not, it's being forced that is the issue.

Such rank hypocrisy is also demonstrated with the so-called "lotteries." When non-bureaucrats "ran the numbers" it was a vicious crime against humanity. But, have a politician do the *exact* same act under a new label such as the "lottery" and now it's a great benefit for mankind. A little political voodoo magically transforms a heinous crime into a harmless beneficial service. Yeah, "What wonderful magic."

And what about "overturned convictions?" A man is put on "trial" and then "convicted." His "conviction" is deemed "legal." If it is "overturned" on appeal, then the "conviction" is no longer "legal." Magic! Nothing has changed except the label attached.

An opinion is just a label attached to the facts.

How is an "opinion" merely a label? Let's say I scream, "I'm going to kill you!" I then pick up a chair and break it over your back. *Those are the facts.* When a lawyer calls that, "assault and battery," *that is an opinion.* However, regardless of the opinion or label attached, the facts will not change. Like it or not facts will not change to fit an opinion. Label it "rape," if you like. *Who cares*? The facts are still the same: I screamed I was going to kill you and broke a chair over your back. You can call an orange a diamond, but that doesn't make it any less an orange.

No amount of human deletion, distortion, and or adding to reality is ever going to change reality.

So the "cop" formed a "legal" conclusion I was within the "state" or a so-called "city" and subject to his "jurisdiction." Fine, I don't fight or argue with him, I just ask him to tell me what *facts* he bases his opinion on. This opinion is no different than if he accuses me of being the Easter Bunny or he thinks I'm a flower. If his accusation is not based on facts (reality) then it's his fantasy.

Fantasies held by majority vote are still fantasies.

This may be hard to accept, *but human deletions, distortions and add-on's are not real.* And this fact does not change just because someone wears a badge or a robe or threatens physical violence.

In my experience, I haven't found one single "cop"

who knew what a "state" or a "city" was; nor have any been able to tell me what "jurisdiction" is. Yes, they will *kill* me, if "necessary" to get me to *acknowledge* and act on these ideas, but ask them to tell you *what it is* and they run to their fellow bureaucrats like "judges" to bail them out.

If a "cop" cannot tell me what "jurisdiction" is he cannot prove his case "beyond a reasonable doubt." Yeah, yeah, I know. It's not the "cop's" *job* to do that. It's the "state" persecutor's job. I've had lawyers snarl this at me a few times. However, in doing so they forget their *entire* case is built upon the "cop's" testimony. It follows that if the "cop" is unable to do so then the persecutor cannot, unless, of course, he draws from other "witnesses" or the persecutor tries to become a witness himself. And this is effectively what they do; the rules of evidence and fairness be damned.

The beauty of all of this is that, if the "cop" *did* know, and could somehow *prove*, I am "within the state," the "judge" will not allow him to answer because he is a non-lawyer trying to form a "legal" conclusion without having been "authorized" to do so because he is not a member of any "state bar." Also, even if permitted to answer, this does not excuse their use of violence because, being within a pretended "state" does not make coercion and good faith any less contradictory. This is only for sake of illustration anyway because his legal opinions are based upon this or that *fiction* anyway and not upon facts, *tangible, verifiable* facts.

So what is a "city" or a "state?" *According to lawyers and other politicians*, not me, a "city" is a "corporation" to wit:

> "**city.** A municipal corporation of the largest and highest class..." *Ballentine's Law Dictionary*, page 202.

So, a "city" is not a tangible *physical* or geographical -location, such as Tucson, Arizona. Therefore, the "City of Tucson" and "Tucson" are *not* synonymous or *factually identical.*

This is further proven by their own political rhetoric and public relations:

> "1. Incorporation and organization; classification
> Section 1. ***Municipal corporations shall not be created by special laws, but the legislature, by general laws,*** shall provide for the incorporation and organization of cities and towns and for the classification of such cities and towns in proportion to population, subject to the provisions of this article." Article 13, Arizona constitution (emphasis mine).

Notice "cities" are created by "general laws," not bricks, mortar and *labor*.

So what is a "corporation?" A "corporation," as defined by "honorable" lawyers, not me, is just another fiction or fantasy:

> "Today's new rule emphasizes the dominance of the ***corporation, a creature of the legal imagination***. FN2" *State Tax Commission of Utah v. Aldrich*, 316 U.S. 174, 187 (1942) (emphasis mine).
>
> FN2 "***A corporation is defined*** by John Marshall ***as 'an artificial being , invisible, intangible, and existing only in contemplation of law.'*** Trustees of Dartmouth College v. Woodward, 4 Wheat. 518, 636. The New York Court of Appeals has said: ***'A corporation, however, is a mere conception of the legislative mind. It exists only on paper*** through the command of the Legislature that ***its mental conception*** [a delusion is more like it] shall be ***clothed with power.'*** People

v. Knapp, 206 N.Y. 373, 381, 99 N.E. 841, 844, Ann.Cas. 1914B, 243. [Footnote 2] (emphasis mine).

So, a "city" is a "corporation" and a "corporation" is a "mental conception." A so-called "city" is a "mental conception."

A "city" or "state" is a hallucination, or a halluci-Nation.

A "city" doesn't appear to be a physical location any-more, does it? Still think a "cop" knows what he's talking about if he claims I'm within a so-called "city?"

"Look to the letter, you find nonsense -- look beyond the letter, you find nothing." Jeremy Bantham, Theory of Fictions.

When a "cop" claims I am allegedly within a so-called "city," he is not only inconsistent with reality, he's inconsistent with his pretended "law," *see State Tax Commission of Utah v. Aldrich* immediately above. Just because a man with a gun, a badge and an anti-social attitude sees me at some intersection doesn't mean I'm in a "city" does it? No, it doesn't because a "city" is a "corporation" that "exists only on paper" in the minds of the men and women cavorting around as "cops" and so-called "legislators." Now that appears to be "reasonable doubt" doesn't it?

"The idea of a joint, incorporeal being, made up of several real persons, is nothing but a ***fiction***. ***It has no reality in it. It is a fiction adopted merely to get rid of the consequences of facts***. An act of legislation cannot transform twenty living, real persons into one joint, incorporeal

> being. After all the ***legislative juggling*** that can be devised, "the company" will still be nothing more, less or other, than the individuals composing the company. The idea of an incorporeal being, capable of carrying on banking operations, is ridiculous." Lysander Spooner (emphasis mine).

So what does this really mean if a "cop" is claiming, "under penalty of perjury" and "upon reasonable grounds," that I am somehow within a "mental conception?" It means his "reality" and that of the entire pretended "court" *is all in their heads* and no where else. The "cop," "judge" and the persecutor are living in a political dream world they are violently foisting on me and millions of others. Whoa, excuse me, but exactly *where, when, why* and *how* does a man, any man, come within a "mental conception?" If a "city" "exists only on paper," then how did I ever get "within" one *physically*? I never did and I never will. I can only be "in" a "city" ***within someone's mind and nowhere else.*** Did Alice take a *machine gun* and force others to accept *her* Wonderland? If she did would she be hailed as "honorable?"

Let's try, for a moment, to suspend reality and think from the standpoint of a traffic "cop." What exactly are his "reasonable grounds" that I am within his "mental conception?" Remember though, this is "Legal Land" so a "city" does not have to be tangible for a "cop" to "see" me "within" one. Just like all of his other opinions, this one is *all* in his head, a dangerous fantasy or *halluci-Nation*. He has seen me at a certain geographic location, however, he might as well claim he is *Santa Claus* and accuse me of being the Easter Bunny *because he has the same amount of tangible evidence.*

> **In the Real World, hallucinations are not tangible evidence.**

Because, in "Legal Land," *halluci-Nations* and other "mental conceptions" are treated as if they are magically transformed into *tangible evidence,* that is enough for a traffic court "judge" to "convict" someone. After all, there are no rules of evidence or pre-trial discovery in traffic court, at least in "the State of Arizona" and he can be as biased as he wants just so long as he does not "shock the conscience" of his fellow lawyers higher up on the political pecking order.

This is also why I wrote earlier that the phrases such as "State of Arizona" and "City of San Diego" are, *at best,* D/B/A's and alter egos used by men and women who use violence as a way of doing business whether they're *conscious* of it or not.

> **Any title or "office" used by a coercive government "state" agent is merely a D/B/A or alter ego. Strip away that title or fancy "office" and you're looking at men and women who have no more right to control another man than you and I do.**

Take a very close look at what is being written by these lawyers. A "city" is "a mere conception of the legislative mind" that only exists "through the command of the legislature that its mental conception" should be "clothed with power."

Factually, a "legislature" is nothing more than men and women. This means a "city" or "state" is a *figment of their imagination* which other people are then *forced* to accept or at least act on. I may not believe there is a real "city," but because of the violence backing this fantasy by those armed men called "cops," I am forced to act as though a "city" or "state" is absolutely real. *If Alice put a machine gun in your face you'd act as though you were in Wonderland with her too.*

What we have here is a group of individual men and women "commanding" (forcing) other men and women to accept a "mental conception," idea or halluci-Nation. Compare this with what has been said about propaganda and how well it matches what lawyers *themselves* tell us their pretended "laws" really are:

> "***As generally understood, propaganda is opinion expressed for the purpose of influencing actions of individuals or groups*** ... Propaganda thus differs fundamentally from scientific analysis. The propagandist tries to "put something across," good or bad. The scientist does not try to put anything across; he devotes his life to the discovery of new facts and principles. The propagandist seldom wants careful scrutiny and criticism; his object is to bring about a specific action. The scientist, on the other hand, is always prepared for and wants the most careful scrutiny and criticism of his facts and ideas. Science flourishes on criticism. Dangerous propaganda crumbles before it." — Alfred McLung Lee & Elizabeth Bryant Lee, *The Fine Art of Propaganda*, 1939 (emphasis mine).

Could you imagine using the same tactics as bureaucrats to sell lemonade as a kid? Come to think of it, if you sold it the same way you wouldn't really have to have *any actual* lemonade to sell would you? You could just "command" the other children to accept your "mental conception" there was some refreshing lemonade they *had* to buy from you whether they wanted to or not because it was for the "good of the whole" neighborhood. If you were really enterprising then you could allow other kids to do the same by setting up a "licensing" scheme franchise (like "state bars") whereby you could sit back and just collect a cut from each "licensee" in exchange for your "protection" of their exclusive "license" to sell "real" lemonade. The kids could also be told that they had to buy "lemonade" from "licensed" vendors approved by you or they might get cheated because you always maintain strict standards of lemonade purity to "protect" them. This analogy has more similarities to "state" run protection rackets than you may care to know.

"Commanding" me to believe in *any* "mental conception," whether it be a "city" or a "corporation" is really no different than "commanding" me to believe in Santa Claus, the Tooth Fairy or the Easter Bunny. In fact, this is what I see whenever I read "the law" quoted above and notice it does not change the flow of the quote:

> "Today's new rule emphasizes the dominance of the ***Easter Bunny, a creature of the legal imagination***. FN2" *State Tax Commission of Utah v. Aldrich,* 316 U.S. 174, 187 (1942) (emphasis mine).
>
> FN2 ***"The Easter Bunny is defined*** by John Marshall ***as 'an artificial being, invisible, intangible, and existing only in contemplation of law.'*** Trustees of Dartmouth College v. Woodward, 4 Wheat. 518, 636. The New York Court of Appeals has said: ***'The Easter Bunny, however, is a mere conception of the legislative mind. It exists only on paper*** through the command of the Legislature that ***its mental conception*** shall be clothed with power.' People v. Knapp, 206 N.Y. 373, 381, 99 N.E. 841, 844, Ann.Cas. 1914B, 243. [Footnote 2] (emphasis mine, with my addition of Easter Bunny for corporation).

How do you "clothe" an idea with power anyway? It's not the *particular* "mental conception" I am being forced to accept; it's being forced to accept a "mental conception" that's the issue. *Change your perception for a moment;* do you want to be forced to believe in a religion? Would you personally force someone else to believe in your chosen religion? Does your neighbor have the right to force you to believe in a certain religion? To help understand this:

just liken politics to a religion.

It doesn't matter if it's a "city, " state," "nation," the Easter Bunny, Santa Claus, Vishnu, Zeus, Horus, or Muhammad, I don't want to be forced or "commanded" to believe in *anything*. Not only is politics a religion, but the "state" is very much a church and an incredibly violent one at that. If likening politics to a religion is too uncomfortable for you, then think of politics as a mythology *because it is a mythology*.

If you ever wonder if a bureaucrat has the "right" to do something, then just ask yourself this question:

Does my next-door neighbor have a right to do this to me?

If he doesn't, then his pretended delegates, deputies, agents, commissioners, governors, presidents, kings, princes, czars, ministers, secretaries, and servants don't either. It's that simple.

An obvious question here is *why* would any idea, religion, myth or hallucination *have* to be imposed by force? Maybe because that's the only way *rational* people will not only accept the idea, but also to act on the idea as if they actually believe it.

Violence is the means by which the *irrational* get the *rational* to act.

What if, like the "mental conception" called the Easter Bunny, I choose *not* to accept the idea that I'm within a "state" or a "city?" What are the implications? First, it would be safe to assume that no one is willing to murder me because I don't believe in the Easter Bunny. The very opposite is true when it comes to bureaucrats. Bureaucrats actually believe they have a "right" to kill you if you refuse to accept their "mental conceptions," be it a "city" or the Tooth Fairy, *it really doesn't matter.* If you don't believe this read Article I § 2 of the Nevada Constitution, directly below; it is also available online at http://www.leg.state.nv.us/Const/NVConst.html. This is such a gem of political doublespeak and statist nonsense that I have to include it in this book about political myths:

> "All political power is **inherent in the people**[.] Government is instituted for the protection, security and benefit of the people; and they have the right to alter or reform the same whenever the public good may require it. But the Paramount Allegiance of every citizen is due to the Federal Government in the exercise of all its Constitutional powers as the same have been or may be defined by the Supreme Court of the United States; and no power exists in the people of this or any other State of the Federal Union to dissolve their connection therewith or perform any act tending to impair, subvert, or resist the Supreme Authority of the Government of the United States. The Constitution of the United States confers full power on the Federal Government to maintain and Perpetuate its existance [existence], and whensoever any portion of the States, or people thereof attempt to secede from the Federal Union, or forcibly resist the Execution of its laws, the Federal Government may, by warrant of the Constitution, ***employ armed force in compelling obedience to its Authority***." (Emphasis mine).

This is a declaration of war for goodness sake. Here, the "government" is said to serve the people who are of allegedly the power and yet the people cannot peacefully withdraw their support without armed forces compelling obedience. ***Which one is it***? Both cannot be true. How many people do you know that are willing to *kill* their "boss" just to keep ***their jobs***? People willing to kill to keep a job are usually described as psychotic. In legal land they are called "honorable." Is your job so important you feel it's necessary to kill your boss to stay employed? I think normal people just go get other jobs. Instead of a "going out of business" sale, politicians start a "war against unemployment." Can you imagine a political party that might use the following speeches and campaign slogans?

> "Yes Sir, vote for me and, once in office, if you dare withdraw your support, we'll kill every last one of you if we have to! But, vote for me anyway because, the other guy will kill you for a lot less!"
>
> "Vote for me, Joe Bureaucrat, cuz' Bob Bureaucrat will kill you for doing a lot less."

Politicians are not only willing to kill their alleged bosses to keep their *jobs*, some shamelessly *advertise* their murderous intent in their own "constitutions." This type of content is not hidden. You can go into most libraries or look online. It's one thing for a slave to kill the slave monger, but it's quite another for the "public servant" (bureaucrats) to kill their so-called "sovereigns." Just how many are they willing to kill to stay employed anyway? 50%, 75%, 90%??? And keep in mind that Pol Pot probably didn't write that section of the Nevada "constitution."

Think about this: If men, women and *children* do not want to participate in politics (forcing their opinions on others) any longer some bureaucrats will murder as many of them as they have to in order to keep *their jobs*. Is that fair? *Is that sane, killing children just to keep a job*? Is participation in politics *so* important people should be murdered for deciding to opt out and live a peaceful life? *Did you see any mention in that "constitution" about a trial*? Peacefully withdrawing support is treated as worse than being a terrorist for goodness sake; at least accused terrorists get a mock trial before they're shot. Did you catch the contradiction here? What about the fifth amendment and due process? Isn't that by "warrant of the Constitution?" Armed force without the nuisance of a "trial." That's why I write it's not about protection, it's about obedience.

And what about the part about "protection?" Doesn't *that* sound *familiar*? You're going to be "*protected*" whether you want it or not? *And let's not overlook the offer you can't refuse*: "employ armed force in compelling obedience to its Authority." Apparently Luca Brasi *doesn't* sleep with the fishes after all. Maybe the above "constitution" should read:

> All political power is inherent in the people, ***as long as "the people" means bureaucrats***. Government is instituted ***by bureaucrats*** for the protection, security and benefit of the people ***whether they want it or not***; and they have the right to alter or reform the same whenever the public good may require it ***just as long as no bureaucrat is put out of a job***. But the Paramount (***real***) Allegiance of every citizen ***i.e., slave, serf, peon,*** is due to the ***men and women pretending to be a so-called*** Federal Government in the exercise of all its Constitutional powers as the same have been or may be defined by the Supreme Court of the United States; and no power exists in the people of this or any other State of the Federal Union to dissolve their connection therewith or perform any act tending to impair, subvert, or resist the Supreme Authority of the Government of the United States. The Constitution of the United States, ***although just***

> ***a mere written instrument no one ever bothered to sign, somehow*** confers full power, ***how, we don't know,*** on the Federal Government to maintain and Perpetuate its existance [existence], and whensoever any portion of the States, or people thereof attempt to secede, ***i.e., peaceably withdraw support*** from the Federal Union, or forcibly resist the Execution of its laws ***i.e., mere opinions, delusions and fantasies,*** the Federal Government may, by warrant of the Constitution, ***an unsigned written instrument,*** employ armed force ***i.e., shoot men, women and children down, like dogs in the street,*** in compelling obedience to its Authority.

If it's true that all political power is inherent in the people, and they choose to *peaceably withdraw* their support, would they not at the same time be withdrawing their alleged political powers from the so-called "government?" If so, then under what pretense or "Authority" would the "Federal Government" be "exercising?" If the people just didn't support them anymore, then by what *pretended* "authority" would they "employ armed force?"

Getting back to the "mental conception" and its application in my traffic cases, let's say, for example, I am traveling safely down the street without a so-called "license plate" on my car. I am not "speeding" or causing any danger to anyone and a "cop" gets behind me and puts his emergency lights on. The "cop" certainly accepts the "mental conception" or opinion that when his lights are turned on, the person in front of him is supposed to stop. However, like the idea of an Easter Bunny, I don't accept this "mental conception" and continue minding my own business.

What will the "cop" do? More than likely he is going to either threaten me somehow with physical violence or he'll just start using physical violence to stop me on his own. Either way, if I don't stop he will probably increase the physical violence until I am stopped, including calling additional armed troops more commonly known as "backup." Some of their cars may even ram my car.

Once stopped, I will more than likely be approached by several "cops," each pointing a loaded firearm directly at my head. Once their firearms are drawn they are fully prepared to murder (kill) me where I sit. Just ask a "cop" and he'll confirm this. At this point it no longer matters that I didn't have a seatbelt on, no, I have done *far, far* worse. I failed to accept a bureaucrat's "mental conceptions" by stopping. This is usually taken as a personal affront to their "right" to dominate me. Now they're *really* ticked off.

Failing to accept a "mental conception" certainly warrants the use of violence, doesn't it? After all, isn't violence an acceptable way to get people to believe the same as you? Isn't it "legal?" It is in "Legal land."

Let's put this in another context: Obviously, no one can really force me to believe in the Easter Bunny, but I can be forced to *act on this belief* by coloring and hiding eggs at gunpoint, can't I? There is a world of difference between believing something and acting as if you do. Compare this to a traffic "trial" because that's how bureaucrats operate; you don't have to believe there is a "state" but you will perform as though there is one by getting a "license," filing a "tax return," putting your children in "state" run propaganda mills called public schools etc.

For example, a "cop" accuses me or anyone else of being within a "city" and "failing to provide ID." This "cop" might as well accuse me of being in Bunnyland and failing to color and hide eggs. In both cases "mental conceptions" are being used. How should such an accusation (opinion) be responded to, if at all? If there were no physical violence to back it up I would just walk away laughing from this delusional anti-social individual.

On the other hand, if I responded at all I might say, "I'm sorry but I don't believe in the Easter Bunny." The "cop" would probably respond that that doesn't matter. *Only his belief matters because of his gun and his willingness to use it to get me to act as if his fantasy were real.* Regardless of my belief though, he not only believes in the Easter Bunny, he also believes he *represents* the Easter Bunny and, because he thinks I'm somehow in Bunnyland with him, I *must* color eggs and hide them, or get shot. My failure to merely play along with his delusion will result in the taking of my time and money (a "fine"), or could result in my death. And I'm sure statists would not see anything wrong with such a cold-blooded murder and say, "He should have just colored those eggs."

In this context, it's very easy to see the "cop" for what he is. He's a man with a gun expressing opinions with no factual support. And, without facts to support those opinions, his beliefs are pure fantasy. In that case it really doesn't matter if he accuses me of being within a "city" or *Bunnyland* because both are mere "mental conceptions" with no tangible existence outside of the head of the "legislator" to which all of this nonsense can be traced back. And why does the "cop" rely on this "legislative" gibberish? *Because he gets a paycheck, a gun, a neat looking badge and gets to dominate other people with impunity.* On the other hand, there is nothing stopping me from actually believing I'm in Bunnyland and just coloring eggs or paying whatever "fine" the "judge" demands I pay.

However, getting back to the traffic stop, let's imagine they ask me *why* I didn't stop. What could I say to such a question? I could say I didn't realize I was supposed to stop. They could then tell me they put their lights on and I was *supposed* to stop (this is another great example of a "non sequitur"). Then I might ask them why I should stop because they put their lights on. Whatever their response is I could then tell them that, like the "mental conception" (idea) of the Easter Bunny, I don't believe in such a thing. The bottom line here is this:

Bureaucrats use *physical violence to force you*

> ***to act on their*** **"mental conceptions," mere *ideas* in their heads, whether you believe them or not.**

If you don't *believe* this, the next time those magical lights come on behind your car, if you don't want half a dozen or more *loaded firearms* pointed at *your head,* then you'll stop your car. And most people know this is true. Your beliefs are just not important, only the beliefs of the man with the gun are important. I like how Jim Robertson put it:

> "Co-equal decision-making vs. following orders and submission – Bureaucrats follow orders. They believe in giving orders to other bureaucrats. If you are not a fellow bureaucrat, you are even lower in status in their eyes. You need to be told what to do, how to earn your money, how to spend your money, what is safe for you, and so on. **Bureaucrats believe that most people are like children, who need to be told what to do and punished for not following orders**. You respect the viewpoint of others, and their freedom to hold other viewpoints. **Bureaucrats believe only their viewpoint is relevant, and that their viewpoint is an order that you must follow**. You regard no person as your slave, nor any person as your master. Bureaucrats believe that they have authority to give you orders, and that you must be punished if you disagree. They believe your life, money, and body are theirs to regulate and use as they decide. Bureaucrats hate those who respect the viewpoints and decisions of others in a meaningful way." — *How Bureaucrats Think And How To Leap Across Them* by Jim Robertson (emphasis mine).

This leads us to a fundamental question: If physical violence is used to force me to accept one opinion, such as my being within a "city," then why not use physical violence to force me to accept all the other opinions and "mental conceptions" such as the opinion I am "guilty of not wearing a seatbelt" in order to avoid a so-called "trial?" What is the "*substantive*" difference between the two, if any? In other words, why not just drop the pretense?

> **What is the point of *having* a "trial" when violence is the basis of how they interact with you?**

It seems inconsistent at best, that they should use physical violence to make me accept their opinion that I am "required" get a "driver's license" but they still put me through a "trial" to convince me I am somehow "*guilty* of driving without a driver's license." Why not be consistent and use physical violence openly to have me accept *all* of their opinions? A so-called "trial" is unnecessary because bureaucrats *do business by coercive means and do not require my consent for anything they intend on doing*, not according to *me*, but according to *them*.

Before you think this is too critical of bureaucrats and that physical violence is "a necessary evil" to provide valuable services, consider this:

> **When was the last time you were forced to pay the operating expenses for Burger King?**

Probably *never*. Normal people do business on a mutually voluntary basis. You have always been completely free to patronize any other fast food business and to even forego fast food entirely. Do you consider physical violence to be a legitimate method of doing business? Statist theology and those who believe in the church called the "state" do. This is not to say, or to even suggest, that violence under any "flag," political banner, or "crime family" is a legitimate way of doing business. It is not. But, seriously:

What is the factual difference between a "state" and a protection racket?

Don't say, "one is legal, the other is not" because that is not a *factual* difference. That's only a different label: "legal" vs. "illegal." The only real difference is that physical violence is not used as openly because politicians are trying to maintain a pretense of fairness. Indeed, they must maintain a pretense of fairness because it's the only thing separating them from their "non-legal" counterparts. The second, more subtle difference, is that coercive "states" utilize more effective public relations on their victims, starting from childhood, with compulsory tax (theft) funded schools. What would your children think of the mob if they were forced into schools run by the mob from the age of five to eighteen? What did Hitler say about children?

This is why it really doesn't matter whether I am within the "state" or not. The only real issue is the violence used to force me to believe their "mental conceptions" or act as if I do.

Bureaucrats use physical violence to get you to comply. More to the point, they use violence to actually *get you to help them* fleece you because, without your "help," doing their jobs would become virtually impossible. To demonstrate this is true, *consider for a moment what a traffic stop would be like if all I did was peacefully refuse to help the "cop" in any way.* I do not stop the car on my own when the lights come on, I refuse to stand up and be handcuffed, I refuse to walk to their car or help them get me in etc. What would "cops" do in such a case? How much more difficult would their "jobs" be if I simply refused to help them? How much more *violence* would they use? Consider the added manpower that would be needed. I don't *resist* them; I just don't *help* them. After all, they believe the "mental conception" they have the right to control my life and property *without my consent*, right? O.K., *I won't disagree or resist you, but go ahead, do your job now.*

If you don't need my consent then, apparently you don't need my voluntary assistance either.

Imagine what would happen if 100,000 people in any major "city" took the so-called "license" plate off their cars and refused to stop when "cops" put their lights on. This alone could effectively stop traffic tickets from being written.

Bureaucrats don't bother asking for permission but they certainly need the help of their victims. Without it, their violent "adversary system" (as lawyers call it) would collapse under its own dead weight and no amount of new "laws" could change that either if enough people just don't accept their "mental conceptions" any longer. What would the politicians do, pass a "law" making *apathy* a crime? And if they did *who would care*?

> "Evil tyrants require, indeed they depend upon, willing and unwilling accomplices – good people who would never think of harming a soul themselves. Lenin called such people "useful idiots."" *What I Have Learned From The Twentieth Century*, Mike Vanderboegh.

> "From all these indignities, such as the very beasts of the field would not endure, you can deliver yourself if you try, not by taking action, but **merely by willing to be free. Resolve to serve no more, and you are at once freed. I do not ask that you place your hands upon the tyrant to topple him over, but merely that you support him no longer**; then you will behold him, like a great colossus whose pedestal has been pulled away, **fall of his**

own weight and break into pieces." Etienne de la Boetie, *Discourse on Voluntary Servitude* (emphasis mine).

Also, aside from not helping a bureaucrat, what would happen if bureaucrats could not initiate the use of physical violence? How could a bureaucrat such as a traffic "cop" do his job if he could not initiate the use of physical violence? They would have a real problem on their hands at that point in time because *their very jobs depend on violence.*

Jurisdiction is control.

Stripped of all political jargon and legal gibberish, "jurisdiction" is control over men, women and children. It's what groups of men and women pretending to be "governments" do. They "govern" and "govern" is control: "**govern.** To direct and control; to regulate; to restrain; to manage..." *Ballentine's Law Dictionary*, page 530. They violently "regulate," control and dominate other men, women and children. This can be observed even by us "uneducated" laymen.

Think about this for a moment, have you ever *seen* a "government?" Can you hit a "government" with a rock? What exactly *is* "government?" The lay answer is, that is, just the facts: a "government" is one man controlling another without the latter's freely given consent. *Everything* else is just opinions to *justify* violently taking control of someone else's life, viz., slavery under the guise of "protection." Remember the *Yick Wo* case cited earlier?

It would be foolish to deny they control me, at least, to a degree, unless, of course, swift and blinding violence against myself is an objective. If I refuse to cooperate, even peacefully, they will use whatever physical violence is necessary to meet their end goal. If I don't stop my car when the "cop" flips his lights on, he will eventually use his car to stop me. Having done so, he'll run up to my car *screaming* at me to get out with his firearm pointed directly at my head ready to murder not a peaceful human being, but what he now believes is a "criminal" or a "perp." See the sick *irony* in such a situation? The "cop" is the violent one and the guy minding his own business, not harming a soul is somehow the criminal. Yeah, I can hear it now, "He should have stopped his car..." That's right, blame the victim. Reminds me of the lawyer argument that a rape victim should not have dressed a certain way. I guess he had it coming to him.

However, getting back to the "cop" as a witness, I'll also ask the "cop" if he had "jurisdiction" over me during the traffic stop, yes, or no? I also ask what "jurisdiction" is *factually*. The blank stare I get as a "response" is the cue for the "cop's" lawyers to jump to the rescue. To help him out I might also ask him if he had control over me *during* the stop. Despite this being a legal conclusion, the lawyers playing "prosecutor" and "judge" will allow it, and he'll probably answer yes because, if he is without jurisdiction, the case *should* be over. You'd be surprised, no, *shocked*, to see just how far some of these altruistic "honorable" lawyers will go to keep a case from being thrown out. If, however, he is not permitted to answer, I again suggest it may be consistent with the rules of evidence to strike his testimony, including the ticket.

If he testifies that he did have jurisdiction or control, I ask, "did you ask for my permission?" He will *proudly* deny that he most certainly did not. This question is mostly for *psychological* reasons. I want him to assist me in exposing his true violent nature so I pump him up with pride. In fact, I want him to *snarl* back at me with contempt:

> ***I'm a cop you little puke*! I don't need your permission to do anything!**

I want his true nature exposed because it contradicts any pretense of fairness and good faith. If what is being done to me is based upon violence, then it's not being done in good faith and is certainly not fair. Anyone who equates physical violence with good faith has *serious* psychological problems and is not a stable person anyone should try and reason with, even if they are "residents" in "Legal Land." No one can get a fair trial from such a person.

Once it is out in the open that it was not with my permission, nor was this required, I ask him, "O.K., other than physical violence, please tell me, *factually*, the nature and basis of this jurisdiction and exactly *where, when, why* and *how* you *acquired* it." This is not going to be answered and with good reason. One in particular is that he was just beating his chest because he doesn't need my permission to do anything. If he even offers a responsive answer (he won't), then he is looking at being impeached as a witness for his inconsistent testimony. At this point the cross-examination is over and it hasn't lasted more than a couple of minutes.

It is always interesting to ask them at what particular point in *time* this "jurisdiction" was acquired because this will really make the "cop" and two lawyers protecting him to start to think. Was it before he saw me, 100 yards away etc. These questions are very difficult to get out of so the "judge" will probably not permit his sidekick, the "cop," to answer. That's fine because:

> "*** '[a] **denial of cross-examination** without waiver *** would be constitutional **error of the first magnitude** and **no amount of showing of want of prejudice would cure it**.' *Brookhart v. Janis*, 384 US 1, 3 (emphasis mine).

I once had a "cop," in a pre-trial deposition, tell me his "badge" was his "authority" over me. I said, "*Really*, is that piece of metal *magic*? Can I put your badge on and have jurisdiction over you?" What is ironic is that he accused me of mocking him. I wonder if he also believes a "crown" would make him a "king," or a scalpel makes him a brain surgeon?

I may help the "cop" out by asking, "is your "jurisdiction" over me based upon your coercion or based on my freely given consent? If he says, "coercion," I can then ask him, "do you equate coercion with good faith and fairness?" This is a great question I have never had answered because they realize answering would open up too big a can of worms for them.

For example, I worked with someone in Phoenix with regards to a "Department of Revenue" hearing. The woman "representing" the "Director" testified to being qualified to draw legal conclusions and having "jurisdiction" over a friend I was helping. The "hearing officer," a lawyer, agreed. He asked the woman if this alleged "jurisdiction" was acquired by his consent and she answered, "no." He then asked her if she equated coercion with good faith and the "hearing officer" (who also represented the "Director") would not allow her to answer because it called for a "legal conclusion." Huh??? I can always count on a bureaucrat to contradict themselves. ***This is because the outcome is always determined in advance so their actions must conform to that predetermined outcome.*** Remember the "magic bullet" theory of the so-called "Warren Commission?"

Another good question is, "since this jurisdiction is not based on my consent, does it extend to the Cayman Islands?" Think about this for a minute. If his control over me is not based upon my consent then why can't he follow me to the Cayman Islands and control me over there too?

Another good point that you may want to consider is this: If the "cop's" so-called "jurisdiction" is really just coercion and physical violence then it has nothing to do with any so-called "constitution," *a mere written instrument no one ever bothered to sign.*

If I don't accept his opinion he has "jurisdiction" over me, then this doesn't matter does it? He'll just use whatever physical violence is necessary to reach his objective. He doesn't *need* me to agree with him or to even believe him. This has nothing to do with consent and good faith, the way rational people interact with each other. Given that fact, why is a so-called "trial" necessary? My input is irrelevant and not required and he has probably told me this already. What has changed *after* the traffic stop?

This applies equally to the "judge's" opinions. He controls my life without my freely given consent. In other words, his so-called "jurisdiction" is not *based* on coercion, *it is coercion.* I may not believe his opinion that he has any "jurisdiction" over me but because the "cops" at his disposal *blindly* accept that he does, I have to act *as if* he does also or get shot.

Because he uses violence and threats of violence, e.g., a so-called "warrant" for my arrest to ensure my presence in "his" building, then why doesn't he use the same level of open violence to ensure I just pay the fine he wants to impose and just skip the whole damn "trial?" What is "fair" and "just" about violence? It's bad public relations.

As previously stated, bureaucrats must maintain a false perception of fairness and good faith because if they don't they will be seen for who and what they really are. They don't want their true nature to be seen because people would withdraw their support, and no amount of threats, from the Nevada constitution or otherwise, would keep those politicians in power. This is why there are even more lawyers doing business as "appeals courts" who "review" a "judge's" actions to "ensure" that a *pretense* of fairness is maintained by the lower court "judge." That is to say, the trial "judge" used good PR. If not, the case could be sent back ("remanded") back to that "judge." Not to administer justice however, but to make the theft of my time and property *look good.*

This is why I put bureaucrats on the spot. If none of this has to do with my consent, then why is a so-called "trial" even necessary? What is a "trial" supposed to accomplish when they can always force ("command") me to accept their opinions ("mental conceptions") anyway?

Look at the inconsistency here. The following opinions

(lies) are not subject to my challenge or consent:

I must have a "license plate" on my car.
I must stop my car for a "cop."
I must comply with a "cop's" orders.
I must appear within "their" building.
I am within their "state."
I am within their "city."
I am subject to their "jurisdiction."

Then, at "trial," only one opinion *appears* (under their pretense) to be subject to challenge:

> I am "guilty" of not having a "license plate" on my car.

But if I cannot challenge the opinion I need the plate on my car, then can't you see this cruel game is rigged from the start? Can you see the difference between this and a case of rape? In a rape case they are proving a certain act was committed as opposed to proving whether I was obedient to the "written will" of individuals I have never met. What makes this particular opinion any different from the other opinions I was forced to accept? One thing: *the pretense of a fair trial necessary to maintain good public relations*. My "challenge" is *superficial* at best, and for appearance only. That is why the "cop" can throw out opinion after opinion *ad nauseam* and, when I ask him to provide the facts those opinions are based on, *both of his lawyers*, the "prosecutor" and the "judge" will not permit him to testify.

> **If I can be *forced* to accept one "mental conception" then I can be *forced* to accept *any* "mental conceptions" whatsoever.**

The point here is the violence. If they can quite literally

force me to accept, and act, upon the mere "mental conception" that I am "within" a "state" then they can force me to accept and act on the "mental conception" there is a Tooth Fairy and have me place teeth under my pillow as a result.

Your *geographic* location determines which *fantasy* ("laws") you're *forced* to accept.

I know some lawyers might hear that and say, "That's ridiculous to compare a state or a city to the Tooth Fairy. You're mixing apples and oranges Marc." My first response is, what if the *opposite* were true? Is it *possible* that what's ridiculous is labeling a man a "citizen" as if that label *in and of itself* now means this hapless victim no longer has control over his own life and property? That he must also ***pay*** for this "privilege" of being violently dominated? That if he doesn't pay then he'll get locked in a cage? Thinking you may forcibly control another person for no other reason than labeling yourself a "government" and your victim a "citizen" is what is ridiculous. Plainly described, this is unrighteous dominion. The enslavement of men, women and children of African decent was itself a form of "government."

My second response is I have not described a "city" as a "mental conception." No, as shown previously, that was a gang of "honorable" lawyers when I cited a "Supreme Court" opinion called: *State Tax Commission of Utah v. Aldrich*, 316 U.S. 174, 187 (1942). Who would deny the Tooth Fairy is a "creature of the ... imagination?" The Tooth Fairy and a "city" are both "mental conceptions" whether lawyers agree or not. The only *"substantive"* difference between a "city" and the Tooth Fairy is the *lack* of violence being used to force me to accept and act upon the existence of a Tooth Fairy.

Lawyers may look at the *Aldrich quote* and just sneer, "Oh, that is just *dictum* anyway." And who am I to argue with that? *Everything* politicians have is *dictum* and *opinion*; the only difference between dictum is the violence used to ram it down my throat. Lawyers wanting to be "judges" have *dictum envy*. Even the "cop" spews forth *dictum* as well as the attorney with the robe; there is no difference ***except*** for the violence behind each one.

That is why it is so important *not* to disagree with "honorable" lawyers or other well armed bureaucrats. It makes no sense to argue with people who use violence to do business. As the maxim goes, "**contra negantem principia non est disputandum**." In other words, it is useless to argue with one who denies principles.

> **I don't argue. Instead, I *let* them sacrifice either their use of physical violence or their pretense of good faith and fairness.**

A good example was a "court case" I was involved with in Arizona. I arrived at the building for the so-called "arraignment" very early and took a seat beside some friends. I always get there early so I can note the "judge's" demeanor.

Despite being kind and patient with everyone before me, he "lost it" when it was my turn. I handed him a copy of a proposed "plea of guilty." All I had to do was sign it and have the "release bond" (ransom) assigned to cover the "fine." This "judge" went nuts because I said I was *intending* to plead guilty and I just wanted to know the nature and cause of the charges and proceedings. This is the only way a plea of guilty may be accepted under rule 17 of the Arizona Rules of Criminal Procedure: "a plea of guilty or no contest may be accepted only if voluntarily and intelligently made."

He refused to tell me anything and screamed for security to come in. I asked him, "What rules, if any, apply to these proceedings?" This only made him angrier and is probably the reason why the security guard appeared so confused about why he was called and for who. I then asked the "judge," "Do the Arizona Rules of Criminal Procedure apply?" He lost all patience and entered a "plea" for me and told me to "wait for a pre-trial date." I then asked the security guard standing next to me, "What can be done if the judge is breaking the law?" He answered, "Oh, he's the judge, he can do whatever he wants." If you doubt this, then just go to any "court" and ask a "cop" or "security guard" the same question. Then I said, "Really? What if he takes out a gun and starts shooting people?" He replied, "Well, he can't do *that*." I responded, "Great, now we've drawn a line in the sand and we know that he *can't* do whatever he wants, let's see if he crossed the line this time." He was not amused at all.

The last thing I asked the "judge" was, "Is there evidence of a complaining party here?" This was all he could take, his face went crimson and he called the "police" to have me thrown out of "his court." What is ironic is that this "judge" said *I* was a difficult man to deal with. Imagine that, he resorts to violence because I asked a question and, here, I'm the difficult one. Irony, it seems, is not lost on bureaucrats. It's also ironic because "judges" are supposed to be of "good moral character" and keep their jobs through "good behavior." Do you equate "good moral character" with getting violent because someone asks a question?

Another example involved a "judge" that was *not* also a lawyer. Most are. I came in and sat down at the defendant's table with my books. The "judge" suggested I come up to the bench. I said I would prefer to sit at the table where I could take notes. He "flipped out" and started screaming at me to come up to the bench or he would "throw" me in jail. I told him again, "I prefer to sit at the defendant's table." It was at this point in time he noticed my friend Dinah was videotaping him. He screamed at her to stop but she just kept on taping. To my great disappointment we later found out she was not actually recording. The "judge" threw several books at me and then ran off the bench in disgust. It was *hilarious*. I filed a complaint with the typically useless "Judicial Conduct Commission" and this "judge" was "retired." I write "useless" because most complaints to that commission are not taken seriously. It's about as vain and pointless as filing a complaint against a lawyer with the "bar."

There is a good reason why a record is rarely kept in traffic courts. What happens in cases I am involved with never leaves any doubt in the minds of everyone present what is going on, that is, *a really bad dog and pony show*. "Judges" always sacrifice any semblance of good faith and fairness. Each one usually resorts to violence in the first instance:

> "Violence is the last refuge of the incompetent."
> Isaac Asimov, Foundation trilogy, The Mayors
> book 1, part III.

Violence is what happens when a bureaucrat feels they're losing their control and dominance over you. They tend to find this *extremely* frustrating. I've noticed that bureaucrats don't treat people as humans to be reasoned with and certainly not as equals. "Cops" treat people like animals during traffic stops; their victims have no rights and must blindly follow their "orders" or get shot. It's important to keep in mind bureaucrats, especially "cops," are *trained* to dominate and "be in control of situations," or at least to believe they are supposed to be. Just ask any "cop." If they feel they're losing control on a traffic stop they'll call "back up" and threaten to hurt you in order to maintain control. During a "traffic stop" in Arizona I asked the "cop," "Except for physical violence, what is the nature of your jurisdiction over me." His response? He looked real puzzled, stuttered a bit and then "ordered" me to stay where I was and called "back-up." This same individual *swore* I was within a so-called "city" and yet he admittedly didn't know *what* a "city" is. Who would believe the burden of proof in a traffic case is the same as a murder trial i.e., beyond a reasonable doubt. I like what Jim Robertson said about individuals like this:

> "Not being "in control of those we have authority to give orders to" strikes at the very core of their jobs and their reason for living. They

> resent it. ***They believe their purpose in life is to smash an iron fist in the face of anyone who they perceive is "infringing on their right to control you."*** *How Bureaucrats Think And How To Leap Across Them*, by Jim Robertson (emphasis mine).

On a traffic stop, the "cop" *believes* he is in control so I have to do whatever he demands or else. If he wants to see my "license and registration" then I must obey his order without question *or get shot*. After all, he *owns* me and what I *thought* was "my life" is now *his* to control. Just ask any "cop" who's in control during any traffic stop and they'll tell you; it's certainly not the one considered a so-called "perp" that's for sure.

How do you think a "cop" would respond if, instead of *blindly* obeying his orders, I calmly asked, "Excuse me, but I need to establish what my relationship with you is, if any, *before* we go any further." No "cop" or "judge" I have encountered has ever answered this question beyond, "I'm a cop" or "I'm the judge." Another question is, "excuse me, but, do I *have* to obey you and, if so, why?" More than likely he will respond by threatening violence *right away* or "forthwith." He will inform me that he will "arrest" and cage me, excuse me, *take me to jail*. Our "relationship" is based on violence. I am not in control nor an equal. The "cop" is in control and he took that control without my freely given consent.

Seeing how he doesn't need, and never asked for, my consent, what are the *limitations* on the "cop's" actions and why? The "cop" can do whatever he wants with impunity. The only fly in his ointment is his pretense of good faith; his public relations scheme must be maintained. So what you have here is a relationship based on violence that is commonly accepted as legitimate. If it's legitimate for a "cop" to control me without my consent, then can a "cop" ever go too far? Apparently I have no rights at all if he may control me against my will. The question about the relationship is great to ask "cops" while cross-examining them because it'll seem strange to them and will probably confuse them a great deal. It will not be answered. It *cannot* be answered without exposing how they go about their business. Their charade of fairness cannot be maintained with their violent nature. *This question exposes the sham whether the question is answered or not.* That is the beauty of not arguing with them; I don't even need the question answered. Some may argue that "cops" don't need to know such things. I agree; "cops" don't need to know what they are talking about, *unless of course they are being relied on as witnesses.*

I find it incredible that "cops" use violence to stop your car, violence to search your vehicle, violence to take your property and violence to put you in a cage, but, if they fail to read you your "rights" before putting you in that cage, *then* they've done something wrong.

> "Your honor, I was violently ripped from my car, forced to the ground, hog tied, thrown into a patrol car, taken out and beaten within an inch of my life, and put into a cell."
>
> "Officer, when you arrested this punk for not having a seatbelt on, did you read him his rights?
>
> "Yes your honor, I did."
>
> "Looks good to me."

Maybe it's just me, but it appears to be rank hypocrisy to read someone their "rights" while callously *disregarding* every one of them; using violence to stop their car, violence to search their car, violence to take their property and put them in a cage. ***Actually it's cruel***; it's tantamount to putting a knife in someone's back while kissing them. To make matters worse, these same violent individuals then promise you a "fair trial."

This is another example where the words being used are not congruent with the actions taken. If he's taking control over my life and property without my consent, then it's clear this individual does not believe I have any rights, except whatever rights he in his mercy wants to extend to me. This is usually expressed by the "time worn" statist phrase "consistently rejected" by rational people: "you have all the rights the constitution gives you." *Isn't that also true of any slave*? Slaves have as many rights as the master in his benevolence wishes to extend the slave. And exactly *how* does an unsigned written instrument ("constitution") give anyone "rights" anyway? Is my right to life really dependant on a 200 year old "written instrument" no one bothered to sign? That would mean we would all instantly die if the "constitution" were set on fire. Interesting concept. Again, **pieces of paper do not create anything or convey property rights, people do**. The paper and ink, commonly called a "contract" is merely *evidence* that two or more people conveyed property rights to each other and under what terms.

To further prove that bureaucrats think, or at least act as though they own everything and everyone, let's look at the definition of owner:

> "**owner.** One who has complete dominion over particular property. 42 Am Jur 1st Prop § 37." *Ballentine's Law Dictionary*, page 906.

While you may argue a "cop" does not have "complete dominion" over you and your property during a traffic stop, one thing is clear: *you certainly don't*. If you don't have "complete dominion" you are not the "owner." How does a "cop" get his "dominion" over my property? He doesn't ask for permission, after all, he's a "cop," he doesn't need my permission to do anything. It's by violence, either actual or threatened, "express or implied;" he does not ask for consent nor will he wait for it.

If you read "legal" opinions on searches conducted by "cops," lawyers and other bureaucrats claim the "officer was fully within his rights to search the vehicle." How bizarre. The "legal" definition of owner is one who has "complete dominion." If a "cop" has a "right" to search my car, then *he* has "dominion" and I'm no longer the owner. Maybe I'll get lucky and he'll give me my car back or maybe it'll be *forfeited "in the interests of justice."*

> **This is an example of statist nonsense where you *own* the property but you *don't own* the property.**

If the "cop" has "dominion" then *he* owns it so let him make the car payments from now on and not me. Here, take it, it's *yours,* just stop screaming and put the damn gun down. Exactly how did this "cop" *acquire* his "dominion" or his "right" to search my vehicle? Let's see, was it violence or an obscure "written instrument" neither one of us has signed?

Another example is a so-called grand jury "subpoena," let's say for my books and records. If I own the books and records, then I have "complete dominion over [that] particular property." This means for someone else to use my property, I have to give my freely given consent, because I have "complete dominion." Remember if it's not recognized that I am the owner, then a so-called "subpoena" would not be in my name requiring me to bring in the property. Instead, some bureaucrat would just come by and take what he felt was his. Maybe those bureaucrats just want my *assistance* in bringing *their* books and records to the court without having to pay me.

To be consistent with the definition of owner, I should have no obligation to comply with the "subpoena." This is not the case in "Legal Land." If I don't comply, then armed troops will just take me and the books and records. Now if they have the right to use violence to just take what they feel they are "entitled" to, then why the facade of a so-called "subpoena?" In other words:

I own property and DON'T own property at the same time

Maybe the "grand jury" owns the books and records. I guess they could just sell them couldn't they? Why give them back? Some may argue the "grand jury" *needed* my private records for trial "out of *necessity*" as if *their need* somehow terminated *my* property rights, that is my "complete dominion." I hope a "grand jury" doesn't "need" five pints of my blood. There are many people in need of a new kidney, do they just cut a potential donor open and take what they feel they need? After all, "**Necessitas non habet legem**...Necessity has no law..." *Ballentine's Law Dictionary*, page 837. If charged with mutilation, can that person laugh as a defense? "**Necessitas vincit legem; legum vincula irredit**...Necessity supercedes law; it laughs at the fetters of the law." *Ballentine's Law Dictionary*, page 837. What if my "friendly" neighbor *needs* a ride to work? Can he just then steal my car "out of *necessity*." We have a 2003 Lexus here and we have three ways to get you into this car; you can buy, lease or *just take it* if you think it's "necessary." Lawyers would write:

> "By decisional law, the rule of necessity may override the rule of property rights." (Rule 81, Code of Judicial Conduct, commentary for Canon 3E(1).

Maybe the definition of owner should be "amended?"

> **owner.** One who has complete dominion over particular property, ***unless a bureaucrat thinks he needs it***.

However, if property rights are not acquired by need or necessity *privately*, then it follows there is no "authority" to then *delegate* such to an alleged "public" body. A "grand jury" is just eighteen or more individuals who gain no more right to my property only by appending a silly label to themselves. You see, in "Legal Land," it's not just eighteen men and women with the same rights as you and I, *no*, it's a *grand jury with a collective right to steal.* Just delete, distort and add to reality to justify the violent taking of property.

There's no merit to any claim that such an alleged right (necessity) was "surrendered" to the individuals strutting around as a so-called "government" either. If property rights are magically lost through "necessity," then there are no property rights to then hire a "government" to protect and maintain.

Also, if rights are "surrendered" to the "government," then what is left for protection? What an *insane* premise: in order to have your rights *protected* you must surrender them first: in order for you to enjoy those pork rinds, you have to give them to me.

Imagine private individuals doing business the same way bureaucrats do: You want your business *protected* by a security company but, in order to *protect* your business, you first have to *give* the entire business to the security company. Or, maybe, this is not so insane after all. It just sounds that way. If you *have* no property rights, then you have *no rights to be violated* and, if you don't *own* property, then you can't *legally* have anything stolen from you, you see? Again this is "Legal Land" where "logic" is totally divorced from reality.

It's kind of like the "relationship" with the "cop." If it's all ultimately based on violence anyway, then how can the "cop" do anything wrong in a bureaucrat's mind, or in the minds of those who accept their premise? The notion that "the king can do no wrong" is the basis for his so-called "sovereign immunity." So, having said that, try to imagine the same exact "traffic stop" without the emergency lights, the badges, and the costumes. Instead, just the guns, the men and the cars. What would be the difference between that and highway robbery? Only one: not all "cops" accept a credit card at the "stop."

If you accept the premise I *must* perform *any* activities

for this man, such as stopping my car and showing him "traveling papers" *despite* having a productive life to lead, then, what are the limitations on what *else* he may demand of me? If I "must" stop my car, then why not wash his "patrol car" and paint his house also? Since none of this has to do with my freely given consent then why not order me to mow his lawn while we're at it? Why not just "arrest" me and have me scrub toilets at his "police department?" Isn't it a well-accepted "mental conception" that I can be held for twenty-four hours without being "charged?"

> **The issue is not the actual activity forced to perform, it's being forced to perform.**

Remember what the lawyers doing business as a "Supreme Court" wrote:

> "For, the *very idea* that man may be *compelled* to hold his life, or the means of living, or any material right essential to the enjoyment of life, ***at the mere will of another***, seems to be intolerable in any country where freedom prevails, as being ***the essence of slavery itself.***" *Yick Wo v. Hopkins*, 118 U.S. 356, 370 (emphasis mine.)

Doesn't this describe every situation with a bureaucrat, especially on a so-called "traffic stop?" Maybe the lawyers who wrote this silently exempted themselves? Maybe slavery is slavery only if done "without lawful authority."

The point is because the relationship is based on violence there isn't a limitation on what he can do to me *except* maintaining an illusion of legitimacy.

> If you accept the premise a "cop" has a right to control you without your freely given consent, then you are in no position to complain if he

orders you to shine his shoes.

If "cops" started going too far beyond the accepted "norm" on a regular basis their illusion of legitimacy would suffer, and then disappear as more and more people withdraw their pretended or actual support. A case in point is what happened to Haitian immigrant Abner Louima in Brooklyn New York in 1997. A "cop" stuck a wooden stick in his rectum causing severe internal injuries for no other reason than being suspected of a crime. Where were the "state" lawyers crying "sovereign immunity" over *that* one? The king can do no wrong, right? After all, this king was working "on the job" at the time and didn't he have every right to hold Abner against his will? Maybe that "cop" should have hired the "U.S." attorneys who defended Lon Horiuchi, the FBI sniper who killed Vicki Weaver in 1992 by shooting her in the head while she stood in the doorway of her cabin holding her nursing baby in her arms. Horiuchi was on a "government" payroll at the time and *he* "got away with murder" (*lay* sense) so why complain about having a wooden stick rammed in your butt?

Bureaucrats go through a lot of trouble trying to convince people what they do is legitimate. A good example is compulsory attendance in a bureaucrat's propaganda mill commonly referred to as "public schools." From the time we are five we have this nonsense forced on us; we learn to be a good "citizen" starting at age five. How many five year olds know what "allegiance" is? Is it any wonder that so-called "schools" bought and paid for through violence end up having such violent episodes such as the one that happened at Columbine High School?

This BS public relations scheme is why they "give you" a trial, whether you want one or not. It's political sleight of hand that distracts you, this way and that, while they perform their "magic" concealing the *true* basis of their so-called "authority." Like a magician, bureaucrats give you a "trial" to *distract* you from the truth while they conceal the violence underlying it all;

the true and sole basis for their pretended "authority." Then they can say, "you had your day in court, your *equal* protection, and your due process!" "Cops" don't know this, of course. Most "cops" I've met don't know more than what they've been told. But, the higher up on the political pecking order you go, the more "state" agents seem to know. From my experiences, many lawyers *know* "the system" is a sham, especially the "honorable" one's wearing black robes. The majority won't tell you this because it means losing their jobs and all that goes with it (money, power, dominance, prestige, circle of friends, irresponsibility etc.)

The *beauty*, the Achilles heel of this entire scam is that *because* these phony "trials" are so idiotic and contradictory, they can *very easily* be *exposed* for what they are. A "judge" always "sacrifices" one of the two ways by which he operates: either the physical violence behind all their actions or their pretense of fairness and good faith. It's one or the other.

While my questions don't always result in a pretended "case" getting thrown out, it's the most effective method I have seen for exposing these phony "proceedings" for what they are:

Public relations propaganda concealing violence.

Once it is openly revealed the underlying "jurisdiction" is violence, then the entire "trial" is seen as a mere pretense and sadistic sham. And this may be the reason why lawyers and "judges" refuse to permit a "cop" to answer most questions. That's fine, *whatever*, be non-responsive; one of their methods of operation is being sacrificed, the pretense of fairness. That's because although the *entire* so-called "case" is based upon this "cop's" legal opinions, the "judge" will not permit me to question him about the supporting facts. Not being permitted to question the sole witness against me sounds like a really fair trial.

As stated previously, the refusal to permit a cross-examination is about the worst "error" the black robed lawyers can commit, even in "Legal Land." Isn't it interesting that if a "judge" refuses to permit cross-examination and cages me anyway it's just considered an "error," but if I did the same thing it would be a crime?

If the "cop" *is* permitted to testify and he admits our so-called "relationship" is based upon violence, and not on my consent, then the next question is:

Do you equate violence with good faith?

Another variation of this question is, "if our relationship is based on your violence then what does your alleged jurisdiction have to do with the constitution?" And then there is, "are *you* trying to maintain a perception of fairness on a foundation of violence?"

I have never gotten an answer to these questions in any "court" and for good reason. How does one maintain a pretense of fairness while admitting the relationship is based on violence? How do you equate violence with good faith? It can't be done. And that's why any bureaucrat that hears this question quickly realizes he has no case.

To get back to the cross-examination of the "cop," if the "judge" will not allow him to testify, I will ask the "judge," "If he can't testify aren't you *supposed* to strike his testimony?" This puts the "judge" into an *extremely* uncomfortable position. He has *refused* to allow the *only* witness against me to testify and he knows, or *should* know, that the testimony should now be stricken. He also knows by striking the "cop's" testimony he has to dismiss the "case." This means he cannot collect any blood money from me. In spite of that, it's incredible to witness a "judge" *striking* a "cop's" *entire* testimony, including the ticket and *still* refuse to dismiss the case.

There are two main reasons for this: First, the "trial" is subterfuge, political voodoo, and second, according to the "laws" that they've created for themselves, "judges" have no personal accountability. I know the outcome of these so-called "trials" is determined in advance because "judges" *consistently* accept testimony from "cops" *they* themselves determined are not competent to testify. This is done regardless of the geographic location of the "court." Think of the odds that there is no connection here. This is not only grossly unfair, this is also considered an "incurable error," according to their very own "Supreme Courts," even if one excuses the violence underlying the entire proceeding.

"Judges" are not held accountable for their crimes (*lay* sense) as long as those crimes are committed while on the bench "doing their job." *That* is one of the reasons why they just don't care if they make glaring "errors" such as "obstruction of justice." That is also why they will often snap at you, "If you don't like it you can appeal it."

"Judges" have their rulings reversed all the time and nothing is done to them i.e., they are not held accountable or punished in any way, even if a man is sent to jail *maliciously*. "Judges" do not lose a dime of their salary for being reversed. They lose *nothing* when they are clearly wrong and yes Virginia, *it is possible for bureaucrats and "honorable" lawyers to be wrong, dead wrong*:

> "Lastly, the meaning that the Government attaches to Congress' silence in Rule 32 is ***completely opposite*** to the meaning that this Court has attached to silence in a variety of analogous settings." *Burns v. United States*, 501 U.S. 129, 137 (1991) (emphasis mine).

What kind of people want to control others with no personal accountability? Read what this "state" defense lawyer in Phoenix, Arizona, wrote if you still don't believe these lawyers both can and do "get away with murder" every day of the week:

> "The rule of judicial immunity is that judges of courts of general jurisdiction are not liable in civil actions for damages for their judicial acts, even when such acts are ***in excess of their jurisdiction*** or are alleged to have been done ***maliciously or corruptly***. *Acevedo v. Pima County Adult Probation Dept.*, 142 Ariz. 319, 690 P.2d 38" (emphasis mine).

There you have it, lawyers *defending* malicious and corrupt acts even in "excess of their jurisdiction." That would include an Arizona "judge" driving drunk in California wouldn't it? *Would this lawyer defend malicious actions committed against her?* I'll bet this lawyer's reality is dictated by who's paying her. Could you imagine not being able to hold your plumber accountable because he was acting on your behalf when he destroyed your bathroom? What an insane way of doing business don't you think? Immunity and no accountability is SOP for professional parasites.

With their "license" to commit crimes, "judges" *don't have to give a damn* about you and me because they know their fellow "honorable" lawyers will not permit them to be held accountable. It's one thing to not have any respect for human life, but to then take away all personal responsibility while providing a small army and a slew a defense lawyers? Gosh, I guess it's nice to be the "king." This is why, in "Legal Land," "judges" can set aside "their" sacred "constitutional *provisions*" such as:

> "Justice in *all* cases shall be administered *openly* and *without* unnecessary delay." Article II § 11, Arizona constitution (emphasis mine).

This "constitutional" P.R., if it were honest, would actually say:

> Justice in all cases, ***except in cases where judges act in excess of their jurisdiction or are alleged to have acted maliciously or corruptly***, shall be administered openly and without unnecessary delay.

Excusing the underlying violence just to make a point, what kind of service is going to be provided by an individual who knows ahead of time he is going to be paid *regardless* of how he does his job? Add to this the "license" to commit crimes with impunity and what kind of individual do you have? Just what kind of individual actually seeks out such an *exalted* position? Is it really "honorable" to maliciously and corruptly damage people with no accountability? Who do these lawyers think they're kidding?

Could you imagine a *brain surgeon* with the same mentality? Would you go to a brain surgeon who claimed he is "immune" for anything he may do to you during the course of an operation, even *malicious* injuries? A brain surgeon is free to conduct his business in such a manner; however, he'd probably be looking for other work if he were up-front with potential victims. Let's replace judicial with medical and brain surgeons for judges in the above quote from a Phoenix defense lawyer:

> "The rule of ***medical*** immunity is that ***brain surgeons*** are not liable in civil actions for damages for their ***medical*** acts, even when such acts are ***in excess of their jurisdiction, such as injuries to the foot,*** or are alleged to have been done maliciously or corruptly. *Acevedo v. Pima County Adult Probation Dept.*, 142 Ariz. 319, 690 P.2d 38." (my edits in ***bold italics***).

Crazy, isn't it? Especially when you consider how valuable a service brain surgeons provide. If you are familiar with the deposition scene from the movie "Malice," with Alec Baldwin, then you'll *really* understand what I mean.

I know lawyers and other bureaucrats, in defense of their cash cow, may argue "judges" *must* be immune to ensure "judicial independence," "neutrality" and so forth. However, such an argument is "patently frivolous" for at least three reasons:

> 1) *there is no* "judicial independence" to begin with;
>
> 2) to have such alleged immunity, the power had to be delegated to them from the people; and
>
> 3) how does "independence" excuse anyone from committing crimes against the very people they are supposed to be protecting?

Judicial "independence" or "neutrality" is a *myth.* This is because in a "*traffic* case" the "judge" represents the alleged "plaintiff," the so-called "state," and is also paid *by* the "state." That itself destroys *any* claim of independence. The "judge" is also on the same team *as* the "cop" who filed the "ticket" in the first place. They call their team "*the state.*"

Yeah, yeah, I know. Lawyers would gyrate and genuflect in defense of "honorable" lawyers arguing, "Necessity! Necessity!" But that doesn't *make it any less* of a conflict of interest and an unfair trial. I'm sure in his mind, Mark David Chapman felt it was "necessary" to gun down John Lennon... *This only proves a fair trial is impossible and bureaucrats know it,* but they neither respect the rights of others nor their own "laws." *And why should they*? They're "*sovereign,*" remember? They are the new "kings." The very same people who impose the "law" *violently* on others refuse to subject themselves to it. Why? Because *they* would be the first ones *they* would *have to throw in prison* if they had to follow their own so-called "laws." Violent people *not* complying with their *own* rules. Scandalous isn't it? *Shocking*.

On the other hand, if the "judge" were *truly* independent, then he's only an individual violently taking control (so-called "jurisdiction") over my life and property. Remember, no "judge" asks for permission. He has no "legal sanction" for his violence because he is allegedly "independent" and not exercising a "delegated authority."

By definition, someone exercising a "delegated authority" is not independent

What utter nonsense, an *independent* "servant." This doesn't mean I believe the BS that "judges" are "public servants." It just proves it's a transparent lie. What is amazing is this monstrous lie can be told with a straight face. A "servant" is defined as follows:

> "**servant**...***A person employed to perform personal service <u>for another</u>*** in his affairs and who, in respect of his physical movements in the performance of the service, is subject to the other's control or right to control [citation omitted]...***Definitely, one who is not an independent contractor***. 27 Am J1st Ind Contr § 2." *Ballentine's Law Dictionary*, page 1163 (emphasis mine).

Let's not forget the claim by the lawyers D/B/A the "Arizona Supreme Court" to wit:

> "An independent and honorable judiciary is indispensable to justice in our society." Canon 1, Rule 81, Rules of the Supreme Court.

I agree; independence is indispensable to justice, but how is that squared with the claim "judges" are "public servants" exercising an alleged "delegated authority?" It's not; ***they're pathetic lies from a group of men and women incapable or unwilling to tell the truth.*** "Judges" are neither independent nor are they "servants" of the people they lie about "protecting." What does all this mean?

> ***<u>With</u> the pretended "legal sanction" he's not independent and <u>without</u> the "legal sanction" he's a base criminal.***

This is a problem for the bureaucrats. There's no way to resolve this issue, it's a catch-22. The solution? In "Legal Land" it's intimidation, violence and the "time worn" political snarl:

> "If you don't like it just appeal it."

This is a great line to hear especially when review by "appellate courts" is "discretionary."

In litigation without an overt "government" litigant independence is a joke. The "judge" has a political oath of allegiance just as the plaintiff's attorney and the defendant's attorney. How can there be any true independence when the "judge" shares the same exact allegiance with the very same system that's *attacking* you in the first place or *supporting* and *facilitating* the *process* of that attack? Also, if there *is* any such "judicial immunity," in force then *where* on earth did it *come* from? It was either a "delegated authority," as they call it in "Legal Land," or it was "usurped," that's *hallucinated* in the real world.

The political *theory* is that all of the powers exercised by bureaucrats have been delegated to them by the "people." That's where that massive political lie "government of...by...and for the people" comes from. This means that all so-called "judicial power" was delegated by, from, and for the "people." The question is, how many individuals collectively known as "We the People" are considered *immune* from the consequences of their own malicious and corrupt acts? This does not mean I think anyone *should* be immune. This just proves this isn't a delegated power.

On the other hand, maybe there *is* no immunity for so-called "traffic violations" because the immunity that was allegedly "delegated" to these "independent" "judges" was only for malicious and corrupt acts whereas traffic is inherently harmless and innocent. This is an example of what lawyers call:

> "**mala prohibita ...** Wrong only as forbidden by positive law. 21 Am Jur 2d Crim L § 25." *Ballentine's Law Dictionary*, page 767.

This is a "legalese" way of saying: "It's wrong because I said it's wrong." Not surprisingly, because bureaucrats regard "citizens" as (retarded) children (*parens patriae*), this closely resembles what parents often say (yell, usually) at their children:

> **Why? Because I *said* so. Because I'm *telling* you! That's why!**

Think about this inconsistency. You look at the Declaration of Independence and the Arizona constitution and we see the bureaucrat's claim as to *why* the "government" was created. They claim:

> "...governments derive their just powers from the *consent* of the governed, and are ***established to protect and maintain individual rights***." Arizona constitution article II § 2 (emphasis mine).

Well, how do you square *that* with "mala prohibita" laws? If something isn't *wrong* in the first place, then how can making a "*law*" against it be consistent with the alleged purpose of a so-called "government," at least, according to *bureaucrats*?

What about the so-called "crime" of not having ID on you? Whose rights are violated if you walk around without ID? This so-called "law" is not consistent with the *alleged* purpose of the so-called "government." This is just *one more contradiction*; another political lie rammed down our throats at the barrel of a gun.

I've asked politicians if their claim of "jurisdiction" is *factually* consistent with this section (article II § 2) of their constitution and have *never* gotten an answer *except* what I call the "three monkey defense." The reason is obvious. They don't want to admit they have *no* valid case "on the record" or *anywhere* for that matter. This is probably why "judges" threaten violence whenever such questions are asked *as if being violent covers up the fact the proceedings are not fair or is a responsive answer to the question.*

The last point in regards to the myth of "judicial independence," is the justification for violence. Why should a "judge" be immune from liability if he maliciously and corruptly damages the very people he is ostensibly protecting? Who wants to go to court if that's the case? I think they really mean that a "judge" cannot do his job without maliciously and corruptly damaging the unfortunate people in "his courtroom." How would you sell such a service? Imagine a mobster using the immunity defense: "I'm protecting the neighborhood, and to do so effectively, I have to be immune from any personal liability." I guess that's part of the offer I can't refuse.

During a July 2001 "trial," a "judge" in Arizona *sustained* an objection a witness could *not* draw legal conclusions. I walked the "judge," the "prosecutor" and the "cop" through to this point. Prior to this moment, I told the "judge" I only asked for the *facts* the "cop's" legal opinion was based on and Paula sustained it anyway. *Great, this is exactly where I wanted things.* I then put the "ticket" on the bench and told the "judge" if the witness was not competent to testify, then all his legal opinions, including the ticket, should be stricken from the record. I also suggested the entire case should be dismissed so I could go home unmolested. The "judge" denied the request and said the witness was now competent to testify. I said, "*Really*? Ok, then he can answer the question." The "judge" had had enough at this point and said the "cop" could no longer testify and the "cross-examination" was "over." Big surprise there. It was no less a surprise that she didn't care a denial of cross-examination is considered an incurable error, at least, in some parts of "Legal Land."

Here was a classic comedy of errors unfolding in this "courtroom" because the "cop" was going from being considered competent, to incompetent, *back* to competent, and then incompetent once again. This is to be expected when the *opinions* of total strangers are supported by nothing but violence. Contradiction after contradiction is exposed until the "judge" finally breaks down and sacrifices either, one, the use of physical violence or, two, the pretense of fairness.

One or the other has to go. The two cannot co-exist no matter *how* hard the "honorable" lawyer sitting four feet off the floor may try. This is why bureaucrats, like the "state's" lawyer or the "judge," continually try to get me off point by arguing whether I did or did not do the act complained of or just threatening me with contempt for doing *anything* else that deviates from their asinine program. Bureaucrats are also notoriously non-responsive, as if they believe their pretense of fairness and good faith can be maintained by refusing to be responsive.

Recently I helped a friend in California with a problem with the "Franchise Tax Board," or, rather, some individuals forcibly taking (robbing) property under that particular D/B/A. These individuals doing business as the F.T.B. were of the opinion that they had a right to this man's property.

I wrote a few sentences in a letter essentially stating *no position was being taken,* "I am neither admitting nor denying anything at this time ... please provide me with the facts your opinions are based on..." True to form, there was no responsive answer, just another threat of violence from the so-called "F.T.B." I called the number on the threatening letter and was informed this friend had been labeled a so-called "tax protestor" and no response was to be given except of course further threats of violence. This was done despite no *protests* or position of any kind. Who would have *imagined* such a thing: a non-responsive bureaucrat. So here was another clear example that these individuals were *only* interested in taking property *by force* and nothing was going to stand in their way, not even taking the time to answer a few questions from a man who did not even *disagree* with them. Justice is not first on their list, or on their list at all. Lawyers think justice means complying with the "law" no matter what the "law" may happen to be.

> "**justice**...Nothing more or less than exact conformity to some obligatory law." Borden v State, 11 Ark 519." *Ballentine's Law Dictionary,* page 696.

To demonstrate how absurd this is, consider this question, "which came first, justice or the law?" Also, weren't the men hung at Nuremberg complying with German "law?" This of course is not meant as a defense of the atrocities committed in the name of Hitler's so-called "law," it only demonstrates how insane the idea is that justice is conformity to "law."

I spoke to Bernadette with the "Taxpayer's Advocate's Office" in Sacramento, California. This woman told me, *while knowing she was being taped,* there was "no rational basis to conclude the law was being properly applied to" the friend I was helping. Despite having "no rational basis" she adamantly refused to stop the proceedings despite that being her only job description. In addition to that, I had Roger, the "state" agent who did the so-called "assessment" and each of his four supervisors admit *on tape*, there was either no evidence to support the "assessment," or they were not qualified to make an "assessment." Lisa, the top supervisor told me, without a hint of shame or embarrassment, "the law is binding because it's the law." (I don't owe anything because I don't owe anything.) And, to top it off, despite *all* this, the members of the Board of Equalization ("BOE") still believed there was *sufficient evidence* to affirm this so-called "assessment." I guess in California "evidence" *really* means "no rational basis."

My question is *where* is this "evidence?" *The man who did the "assessment" admitted he had nothing.* What is amazing is these bureaucrats gave *no credibility* to the very witness they relied on. The man said he had no evidence and they did not believe him. This experience, and many others like them, taught me that bureaucrats consider their *opinions* to be *evidence* and a substitute for a witness's testimony. After all, they *do* have the guns to get you to comply.

This is why I say a political "law" (as opposed to a *natural* law that is an observation anyway, not the whim of a man) is just an *opinion* backed by a *gun*. This *insane* way of doing "business" is equivalent to having *every* eye-witness to an alleged crime testify they didn't *actually* see *anything*, and still being convicted on *only* their testimony.

"When lies pay better than truth, expect lies."
Unknown.

Chapter Eleven

Conclusion

Have you ever tried to justify a "tax" "assessment" or "traffic" ticket or any so-called "trial" *without* using political words and phrases such as "government," "law," "constitution," "statute," "state," "city," "license," and "jurisdiction?" *Try it;* take a minute and try it. Just use the facts. Describe what "jurisdiction" is factually without using the word "jurisdiction" or the others listed.

In my personal experience no bureaucrat has ever been able to do so and I personally don't think a tax or traffic "case" can be justified, let alone proven "beyond a reasonable doubt," *on just the facts.* This is why bureaucrats *blindside* you with inane legal opinions *ad nauseam,* which means, "to a disgusting extent." *Ballentine's Law Dictionary,* page 36. This gives an appearance, rather, a *pretense* or illusion of validity. But it's still just a pretense; a real flimsy public relations scam. Lawyers appear to not even know the difference between facts and legal opinions as demonstrated by this recent nonsense I received from a Phoenix lawyer:

"STATEMENT OF FACTS

> [Mr. X's] wages and his compensation for services were taxable under the Arizona Constitution and the applicable Arizona statutes, particularly those in Title 42."

Do I really need to point out this is not a statement of facts, but a legal opinion?

The following is another great example of some of the best political nonsense I've read in years. This is from a case in Arizona involving individuals D/B/A the "Arizona

Department of Revenue" (ADOR). These individuals wanted to steal property and put on a proceeding, that in their own words is a complete sham.

The petitioner did not argue with these individuals, he just wanted the facts their opinions were based and they could not provide anything. To justify the decision to continue proceeding against him despite having no evidence whatsoever, a lawyer pretending to be a "hearing officer" wrote the following:

> "The questions the Petitioner posed to the Section's representative were frequently couched in terms of "what is the factual basis for..." To respond to the questions would have required the Section's representative to cite to the law, draw legal conclusions or make legal arguments. Repeatedly the Petitioner was instructed he could only ask questions that would elicit facts."

No, when asked for facts, the response from an honest person is to provide facts, not more legal opinions. Read the quote again and ask yourself if that is the thought process of a normal, healthy adult. What does this say about the people who actually look to this lawyer as some kind of "authority"?

This constant barrage of "legal" gibberish you encounter once you enter "Legal Land" is not unlike Alice's experience once she enters Wonderland because, both here and there, words mean whatever a bureaucrats says or thinks they mean:

> "No, no, no. We're not *stealing* your car. We're *taxing* you." "This isn't *slavery*. It's called *selective service*." "You're not being held against your will. This is an *investigative detention*." "You are free to earn a living and support your family doing *whatever* you want, just as long as you have a license for it."

In "Legal Land," words have no concrete meaning like

we use in the real world. In "Legal Land," bureaucrats make words mean whatever they want them to mean "on a case by case basis." Legal Land is where rocks are roses, dogs are cats, white is black, black is white, cold-blooded murder is "acting within the scope of his employment" and armed robbery is "taxation." For example, the Arizona "constitution" restates the Declaration of Independence's basic principal with regards to "governments" governing "by consent" which bureaucrats *interpret* to mean "majority consent" instead of the obviously correct *individual* consent.

> **When they said "by consent" they *meant, their* consent, not yours.**

Couldn't that also be said of any race that was enslaved by this or that foreigner? Those prospective slaves never actually gave their consent, some slave monger did. This point has an even broader application:

> "It is well-established that before a binding contract is formed, the parties ***do not* have to mutually consent to all material terms**. *Hill-Shafer Partnership v. Chilson Family Trust*, 799 P.2d 810, 814, 815 (emphasis mine, underlined words are my edits).

Can you just *imagine* if the above "precedent" was twisted in order to say that instead. Well, when it comes to bureaucrats, it *has* been. They say "citizens" have formed a "social compact" (contract) to do or not do this or that as part of their "civic duty." The problem is politicians provide *no* evidence of anyone ever actually *agreeing* to do *anything*. I had an IRS lawyer tell me there was a ***real*** "social compact." I asked him what "social compact" he planned on entering into evidence and he told me the "US constitution." I asked him if he was now claiming the constitution was an agreement. His response?

"No, that's not what I'm saying." Really, then what was this lawyer saying? I guess the law dictionaries are all wrong:

> "**compact.** Noun: A contract, Green v Biddle (US) 8 Wheat 1, 92, 5 L Ed 547, 570; particularly, a contract of an important and serious nature..." *Ballentine's Law Dictionary*, page 232.

This IRS lawyer named Richard, didn't know what he was saying. *Apparently he is capable of spewing forth legal jargon faster than he can comprehend it.* And to think most people would consider this lawyer an "authority" on the "law."

Maybe there *are* people (call them "bureaucrats" or something else) that have the power to bind *others* to contracts or pieces of paper that aren't contracts. But, if there *are* (those who can, for example, consent to a "constitution" *for* me), then why don't they consent to all sorts of *other* things for me; such as my participating in Amway or even this or that religion? *What is the limit of their vicarious consent*?

Another example of how bureaucrats use legalese and political language in an effort to bring about a different, or "*alternate*" reality is with the act of stealing. The *lay* meaning of stealing is:

> "**steal**...to take another person's property without right or permission, to take dishonestly." *Oxford American Dictionary*, page 897.

Now, compare that with the "Legal Land" meaning:

> "A person commits theft ***if, without lawful authority***, such person knowingly: 1. Controls property of another with the intent to deprive him of such property..." Arizona Revised Statutes § 13-1802 (emphasis mine).

Maybe it's just me, but doesn't it look as though this so-called "lawful authority" grants bureaucrats a *license* to steal. In the *lay* sense theft is theft, but not in the *legal* sense. In the "legal" sense, if you *do* have "lawful authority" you *can* control the property of another with the intent to *deprive* them of that property. In other words, theft with "lawful authority" is *magically* not theft. What complete and utter nonsense. In the lay sense it's a dog, but *legally* it's a diaper. If it isn't theft then what is it?

Politicians are coming right out saying "lawful authority" is their "license" to steal. That is what a "license" is; the permission to do something that, *without* the "license," would be considered a crime. Sometimes, it really pays off to just *pay attention* to what lawyers and bureaucrats are telling you. Pay close attention to what politicians themselves say:

> "**license** ... The privilege conferred by a public body on a person for the doing of something which otherwise ***he would not have the right to do***. 33 Am J1st Lic § 2." *Ballentine's Law Dictionary*, page 736 (emphasis mine).

So, to them, theft is wrong *unless* you have a "license" to do it, which they call "lawful authority." Read again how Lysander Spooner put it:

> "If taxation without consent is *not* robbery, then any band of robbers have only to declare themselves a government, and all their robberies are legalized." Lysander Spooner, *Letter to Grover Cleveland*.

To demonstrate further this same exact type of "legal" gibberish, I've placed the following two "statutes" from the Arizona Revised Statutes ("A.R.S.") side by side for comparison;

read them very carefully:

"13-1405. Sexual conduct with a minor; classifications.

A person commits sexual conduct with a minor by intentionally or knowingly engaging in sexual intercourse or oral sexual contact with any person who is under eighteen years of age."

"13-1407. Defenses.

A. It is a defense to a prosecution pursuant to sections 13-1404 and 13-1405, involving a minor, if the act was done in furtherance of a lawful medical practice."

A "lawful medical practice?" To have sexual intercourse with a minor!? What are they saying? That it's O.K. if a doctor does it? Did you notice that word "lawful" again? Before anyone accuses me of taking this out of context or somehow misinterpreting this to mean something other than "it is not a 'crime' to have sexual intercourse with a minor if the perpetrator is a doctor," please reference the following:

> "A. A person commits unlawful imprisonment by knowingly restraining another person.
> B. In any prosecution for unlawful imprisonment, it is a defense that:
> 1. The restraint was accomplished by a peace officer acting in good faith in ***the lawful performance of his duty***..." A.R.S. § 13-1303 (emphasis mine).

Notice this is *also* a "state" granted "license" to falsely imprison someone. Apparently these "legislators" believed there are "lawful medical practices" involving adult male doctors having *sexual intercourse with children*:

> "3. "Sexual intercourse" means penetration into

> the penis, vulva or anus by any part of the body or by any object or masturbatory contact with the penis or vulva." A.R.S. § 13-1401.

The issue of "lawful authority" to do this, that or the other thing presents yet *another* contradiction. If a person has *no* inherent right to do something, such as theft, the forcible taking of another's property, then it stands to reason that he gains no right to do so by getting together with some of his neighbors who don't have any such "right" either.

It is self-evident there is no "collective right" to steal. If the whole body of people in a given geographical area were to get together and agree on *any* issue, they still wouldn't have any "collective right" to steal because each person only brings with him his *individual* rights. It's a basic mathematical principal that the whole is equal to the sum of its parts except in "Legal Land."

> **In "Legal Land" two plus two is whatever a "legislator" "commands" you to believe.**

Without an individual right to steal, there is no so-called "collective right" to steal. Without a "collective right" to steal, there is no "right" to then delegate to another body, whether that body is labeled public or private. Because no such body has any "right" to steal, no "license" may then be "conferred" by that body to any so-called "state" agent. It also follows there is no alleged "lawful authority" to steal.

Now, having said all that, let's take another look at that "statute" where bureaucrats in fact succeed at "legalizing" theft:

> "A person commits theft ***if, without lawful authority***, such person knowingly:
> 1. Controls property of another with the intent to deprive him of such property..."

— Arizona Revised Statutes § 13-1802 (emphasis mine).

So what *is* this alleged "lawful authority?" This "lawful authority" is nothing more than violence and threats of violence organized under a pretense of good faith and fairness. Remember, a "law" or a "statute" is nothing more than an *opinion* backed by a gun.

This presents yet another contradiction when placed side by side with the "senate" opinion shown earlier stating that there is no "so-called private ownership of property." If you don't own the property, then it's not being stolen from you, but from the bureaucrats who believe they own everything anyway. Perhaps this would help to explain why theft cases are brought in the name of the "state."

When I am *allegedly* "within the state" I am in "Legal Land" where words can and do mean whatever a bureaucrat needs or wants them to mean. This is why law dictionaries are constantly being revised:

> ""A word is not a crystal, transparent and unchanged, it is the skin of a living thought and may vary greatly in color and content according to the circumstances in which it is used," wrote Justice Oliver Wendall Holmes in Town v. Eisner, 245 US 418, 425 (1918)." Foreword to Ballentine's Law Dictionary, Third Edition.

Really? Maybe it's just me, but if a person uses the word "raisin" to describe a "cat" he's not hailed as a scholar, but is called an *idiot*.

> "Yes, the jury *technically* found you "not guilty," but, in the *legal* sense you are *still* "guilty."

If I accept what Mr. Holmes wrote above, then how

could I enter into a contract? How could there possibly be a meeting of the minds? How about certainty with the "law?" What's the point of having any "precedent" when words mean whatever they want them to mean? This brings up yet another contradiction.

The following is a declaration from a group of men and women strutting around as so-called "legislators" in Arizona:

> "It is the declared public policy of this state and the general purpose of the provisions of this [criminal] title are:
> 1. To proscribe conduct that unjustifiably and inexcusably causes or threatens substantial harm to individual or public interests;
> 2. To give fair warning of the nature of the conduct proscribed and of the sentences authorized upon conviction..." A.R.S. § 13-101.

How can there be "fair warning" when the words used are the "skin of a living thought and may vary greatly in color and content" depending on the context? Remember what lawyers have declared:

> "By decisional law, the rule of necessity may override the rule of disqualification." (Rule 81, Code of Judicial Conduct, commentary for Canon 3E(1).

In other words, the written word ultimately means *nothing* to bureaucrats and lawyers *unless* it is being used as a justification for stealing property in the name of a non-existent "state." If a "law," "statute," or "rule" gets in their way, they "override" it, claiming "necessity," and continue with their raping, pillaging and plundering.

This happened in an "IRS" case in Arizona. The "IRS" lawyer *admitted* the agent had stolen this man's property through fraud. In addition, they admitted that none of the so-called "statutes" governing "assessments" and "collections" were followed. This "US attorney" argued the "IRS" was not *required* to follow the assessment and collection statutes laid out in "Title 26" of the "United States Code" and yet enjoyed "absolute immunity" for crimes committed while on the job. What happened to 26 USC 7214, the "statute" making it a felony for revenue agents to oppress, extort and not comply with the so-called "revenue laws?" That's right, "by decisional law..."

Another lawyer, this one pretending to be a federal district court in Arizona, agreed with this nonsense so an appeal was made to *other* lawyers doing business as the "Ninth Circuit Court of Appeals." True to form, those lawyers also agreed the "IRS" is not required to follow the assessment and collections statutes of "Title 26" of the USC Is it any wonder this opinion was then labeled by these same lawyers as "not to be published, not to be cited as precedent?" Welcome to "Legal Land."

Another bureaucrat from California vehemently claimed, "We have a valid assessment against [Joe Schmoe] Marc!" I responded, "O.K., how many elements are there in a valid assessment?" This not only took the wind completely out of her sails, but it abruptly ended the conversation because she couldn't answer this easy question. Instead, she refused to try to answer and asked me to put the question in writing. She also promised she would be responsive and so I sent her the letter. She then sent me a form letter *four months later* containing nothing but inane ramblings about the "constitutionality" of the "tax laws" and other non-responsive legal mumbo-jumbo. So I called her and asked why she was not responsive to my questions and she said, "Because your arguments were frivolous and completely lacking in merit, they're *ridiculous.*" I responded, "Susan, there were *no arguments*, just a few questions you *asked* me to put in writing which you *promised* you'd be responsive to." She stuttered and finally said, "Well, your *questions* were frivolous." I had to ask her, "Susan, *how* can a question be frivolous?" For some reason Susan couldn't or wouldn't answer me. It didn't matter that she had *asked* me to send them to her. To a bureaucrat *anything* other than a complete surrender to their pretended "authority" is considered "frivolous."

"Frivolous" means "so *lacking* in merit as to require *no* demonstration." So why would she feel compelled to send me a form letter at all? Susan claimed there was a "valid assessment" so I didn't argue or disagree. Instead, I asked her how many elements there were to a "valid assessment." If she is so confident there is a "valid assessment" then she should have been able to tell me how many elements there were. I hardly think such a question was "frivolous." I don't think *any* relevant question is frivolous given its definition. It's not the question that's frivolous, it's the nonsensical bureaucratic answers, *if any answers at all*. However, this was "Legal Land" where the bureaucrats are *always* correct and the non-violent productive people they are fleecing are *always* wrong.

Because of that, if I ever want to make a bureaucrat uneasy, I ask them *if* it's *possible* their opinion *could* be wrong. Not that it *is* wrong, just the *possibility* it could be wrong. This typically produces an emphatic "no" on their part. However, it sets up a contradiction in a situation like the one above with Susan. They are super confident they *cannot* be wrong, ***ever***, and yet they adamantly refuse to discuss the facts to support their legal *opinions* which is classic "Legal Land." Let's just do away with those pesky little facts now shall we?

I called another California bureaucrat recently and told her I was *not* admitting or denying anything at this time. I only wanted to know the *facts* her legal opinions were based on. She said, "Well Marc, the *law* says…" I cut her off and told her I was not interested in what the *law* says, I just wanted to know the facts her *opinions* were based on. She again said, "the *law* says…" I had to cut her off yet again and repeated I was *not* interested in any more legal opinions, just the facts. This comedy routine continued another two times until she finally gave up and said she had "no idea what you're talking about Marc." I would say she was really *admitting* she had no idea what *she* was talking about. The good news is, at least in *that* case she had enough sense to drop her pretended claim.

In my experience most bureaucrats don't drop groundless cases *even when they admit they have no evidence.* This is because bureaucrats have plenty of heavily armed troops on the payroll and are always *long* on opinion and *short* on facts and they *don't* like to be questioned. They especially hate being questioned on their phony "authority," their alleged right to dominate other men, women and children. In "Legal Land" the opinions and "mental conceptions" held by bureaucrats are *the* "law" and those opinions are *never* incorrect. *If you don't believe me then ask a bureaucrat who intends on taking your property and time.* That's why *any* challenge from any *productive* person is labeled "patently frivolous," "specious," or "spurious." Only in "Legal Land" can a *question* be a "groundless legal argument" and "frivolous." I've *wondered* if there is a certain *school* for "U.S. Attorneys" where they are actually *taught* to respond to "IRS" challenges each and every time with just "the petition contains nothing but frivolous legal arguments..." no matter *what* a petition *actually* says. I write this because I've seen this so many times.

Only in "Legal Land" can you *own* property and *not* own property *at the same time.* Only in "Legal Land" can you be forcibly taken *out* of your car, forcibly handcuffed, taken away *against* your will and caged for a ransom while *simultaneously* being read your "rights," as if you had any they gave a damn about. Only in "Legal Land" is it possible to have a so-called "fair trial" based entirely upon violence where the so-called "independent" and "impartial" "judge" not only represents both the very same party bringing the charge and the defendant, but also testifies against the defendant as if he were a real witness. Only in "Legal Land" would children be mercilessly gunned down for doing absolutely *nothing* except peacefully withdrawing their actual or pretended support of the mythology known as politics. And last, but not least, only in "Legal Land" is violence equated with good faith and fairness; where violently taking control of another human being does not "offend traditional notions of fair play" if you label such violent act "jurisdiction."

Lawyers and other bureaucrats whose very jobs depend *entirely* upon violence (they *do* call it the "adversary system") will probably defend their jobs tooth and nail, but that is to be expected. After having spoken to many bureaucrats and researched their "laws" and court opinions, I'm probably familiar with most political justifications for organized violence. It is very rare for me to hear or read about a justification for the violence that surprises me, although I did get a new one recently (summer 2002). This was in the same opinion mentioned earlier where three California "court of appeals" lawyers justified a denial of cross-examination by *presuming* there were even more witnesses the man I was helping could *not* cross-examine.

These lawyers justified the refusal of the trial court "judge" to take "*mandatory*" judicial notice of facts. To do so, they really pulled out the legal absurdities all over again. First, they mislabeled the facts as "legal opinions" and stated the trial "judge" had no obligation to take notice of legal opinions. Then, in a footnote to this dementia, they claimed that, based on this "reasoning," there was no obligation to take notice of these "facts." Try and follow their "Alice in Wonderland" like gibberish here again:

1) A "judge" is asked to take judicial notice of certain facts.
2) Lawyers label these *facts* "legal *opinions*."
3) Judicial notice does not need to be taken of legal *opinions*.
4) Because of this, judicial notice of these *facts* is not required.

Only in "Legal Land" can facts become "legal opinions" and then go back to being facts all over again within the same opinion. This is so a host of lawyers acting as "judges" can ignore the truth and contradict their own rules and sacred "laws." In the real world such actions can get you committed in a "mental institution" as *insane*, but, in "Legal Land," you are hailed as an "officer of the court," a scholar and "honorable."

It's not surprising these three lawyers pretending to be "judges" didn't want their written "legal" opinion published so that it might be cited as so-called "precedent." That, however, will not stop me from making it available for others to read and expose it for what it is-*legalistic gibberish.*

Speaking of legal gibberish, Richard, the lawyer I mentioned earlier recently wrote the following which is typical of lawyers defending the IRS:

> "Examples of the ***irrational legal theories*** and requests of petitioner may be found in all documents sent to the respondent, one of which (the "Petitioner's Requests for Admissions") was attached to the Motion to Dismiss and is also attached hereto as Respondent's Exhibit 1. See for example, Requests 14 ("***The United States government is just a group of men and women***")..." (Emphasis mine).

Irrational? Then what is the "United States government" then? *Reptiles, sharks, leeches*? Obediently surrender 40% of the money you earn and don't you dare question *who* or *what* you are paying it *to*. This same lawyer, who thinks it's "irrational" to consider the "United States government" as men and women is so worried about having to make such an admission or *denial* he'll seek a "protective order" instead of making a simple objection. Normal people just deny the admission. And what does this lawyer mean by "irrational?" My law dictionary defines "rational" as "Capable of reasoning; sane." *Ballentine's Law Dictionary*, page 1057. I would guess that *insane* was what he probably had in mind. He thinks it's insane to believe the "United States government" is a group of men and women. Let's not consider simple, everyday *observation* here for a moment, let's look at what politicians call "organic law" to wit:

> "We hold these Truths to be self-evident, that all Men are created equal, that they are endowed by their Creator with certain unalienable Rights, that among these are Life, liberty, and the Pursuit of Happiness. That to secure these Rights, ***Governments are instituted among Men***, deriving their just Powers from the Consent of the Governed." Declaration of Independence of July 4th 1776 (emphasis mine).

I'll let you decide who the "irrational" one is. To help make this decision easier, let me give another example. This same "IRS" lawyer also claimed the following is an "irrational legal theory" to wit:

> "The Constitution is a written instrument."

Who am I to disagree? I agree; in one sense this lawyer is correct. However, in his zeal to label everything "irrational" so his cronies could steal someone's property, he neglected to check the *source* of the statement. Again, forget about common everyday *observation* to prove the "Constitution is a written instrument" and consider *I didn't write the statement;* I only *quoted* it without the source which just happens to be the "honorable" lawyers doing business as the "United States Supreme Court" to wit:

> "The Constitution is a written instrument." *South Carolina v. United States,* 199 US 437 at page 448.

Think about what this lawyer is really saying. Bureaucrats consider these "opinions" to be the "Supreme Law of the Land." This *lawyer* wrote the "Supreme Law of the Land" is an "irrational legal theory." Why would I disagree with a lawyer who's starting to see eye to eye with me? I would like to hear him explain how some "irrational legal theory" creates obligations.

The last example some people may accuse me of making up; however, it's true and was written by a lawyer representing the "IRS."

This is also part of a request for admissions that was directed to several IRS employees who are material witnesses in a court case: "I have a duty to correctly apply the IRC." They were to either admit or deny this. As stated previously, their lawyer claimed this was an "irrational legal theory..." Why does this experienced lawyer think this? Who knows, maybe he thought I, a mere layman, wrote it. However, all I did was paraphrase the following from some pretended "Commissioner of Internal Revenue:

> "The function of the Internal Revenue Service is to administer the Internal Revenue Code...it is the duty of the Service to carry out that policy by correctly applying the laws enacted by Congress." Internal Revenue Procedure 64-22.

Thinking the "IRS" has a "duty...to...correctly..." apply the "law" is an "irrational legal theory." Do you think the men and women D/B/A the "IRS" have a duty to correctly apply the "law?"

In "Legal Land" bureaucrats get away with saying, "black is white and white is black" because of the violence backing their opinions. In light of this, how can anyone expect a fair trial when a so-called "judge" calls facts opinions and opinions facts? And, to make matters worse, it's *not* that they don't really know the difference, it's done *deliberately*.

Don't expect fairness from the agents of any coercive "state" because to them we are cows to be milked. If you doubt this, then consider the following gem of political nonsense sent to me by a close friend in Australia (thanks Mate). If this doesn't convince you that politicians are violent and delusional, then nothing will.

This is from section 165-55 of the GST (goods and services tax) ACT of 1999:

> "For the purposes of making a declaration under this Subdivision, the Commissioner may:
>
> (a) treat a particular event that actually happened as not having happened; and
> (b) treat a particular event that did not actually happen as having happened and, if appropriate, treat the event as:
> (i) having happened at a particular time; and
> (ii) having involved particular action by a particular entity; and
> (c) treat a particular event that actually happened as:
> (i) having happened at a time different from the time it actually happened; or
> (ii) having involved particular action by a particular entity (whether or not the event actually involved any action by that entity)."

A delusion is defined medically as "false beliefs that usually involve a misinterpretation of perceptions or experiences." *The Merk Manual of Medical Information*, page 436. That is exactly what is being prescribed in the "GST" above.

That leads me to conclude politicians/bureaucrats are schizophrenic:

> *"Schizophrenia is a serious mental disorder characterized by loss of contact with reality (psychosis) hallucinations, delusions (false beliefs), abnormal thinking, and disrupted work and social functioning." The Merk Manual of Medical Information,* page 435.

Pretending something exists when it doesn't qualifies as being schizophrenic; and it's no coincidence it's also the "Commissioner's" job. Add a willingness to kill a man based on delusions and you have a real psychopath on your hands.

Yet, such people are hailed, worshiped or revered as so-called "authorities." Maybe that's why Einstein said, "Unthinking respect for authority is the greatest enemy of truth."

> "The fact that an opinion has been widely held is no evidence whatever that it is not entirely absurd, indeed, in view of the silliness of the majority of mankind, a widespread belief is more likely to be foolish then sensible." Bertrand Russell.

Chapter Twelve

Final thoughts

This book shouldn't end without some explanation of an alternative to a coercive "state" and the mythology supporting it. People only need to provide better services and products than bureaucrats do. This in a sense could put them out of business; to finally and forever put to rest the nonsense that services need to be provided on a compulsory basis. It doesn't take violence to put this dinosaur called politics to rest; apathy and better services provided on a mutually voluntary basis can. As you can tell I'm no fan of coercive business practices. I am sure you would agree that no service or product should be administered at the barrel of a gun.

However, I don't need to reinvent the wheel; there are many books already out dealing with this subject and I highly recommend the writings of Murray Rothbard and in particular *Sic Itur Ad Astra* by Andrew J. Galambos.

Maybe you've never looked at what a so-called "government" does as a service or product before. Isn't that all these men and women are *supposed* to be doing? They weren't hired to be self-appointed gods, were they? What else is meant by the Declaration of Independence?

> "We hold these Truths to be self-evident, that all Men are created equal, that they are endowed by their Creator with certain unalienable Rights, that among these are Life, Liberty and the Pursuit of Happiness. ***That to secure these Rights,*** Governments are instituted among Men, deriving their just Powers from the ***Consent of the Governed.***"

Protecting "life, liberty and the Pursuit of Happiness" is

a *service* provided by men and women like you and me. *There's nothing magical or special about it and there is nothing indicating this type of service should be **canonized** and administered at the barrel of a gun.* Lysander Spooner put it this way:

> "If A were to go to B, a merchant, and say to him, "Sir, I am a night-watchman, and I insist upon your employing me as such in protecting your property against burglars; and to enable me to do so more effectually, I insist upon your letting me tie your own hands and feet, so that you cannot interfere with me; and also upon your delivering up to me all your keys to your store, your safe, and to all your valuables; and that you authorize me to act solely and fully according to my own will, pleasure, and discretion in the matter; and I demand still further, that you shall give me an absolute guaranty that you will not hold me to any accountability whatever for anything I may do, or for anything that may happen to your goods while they are under my protection; and unless you comply with this proposal, I will now kill you on the spot," —- if A were to say all this to B, B would naturally conclude that A himself was the most impudent and dangerous burglar that he (B) had to fear; and that if he (B) wished to secure his property against burglars, his best way would be to kill A in the first place, and then take his chances against all such other burglars as might come afterwards." Lysander Spooner, *Letter to Grover Cleveland.*

Consent means consent, *individual* consent. If the Declaration did not mean individual consent, then the Declaration is nothing more than political rhetoric and not worth the paper it's written on. Consent means you are free to accept the service or not, without conditions attached or coercion of any kind.

Some may argue there *must* be compulsory payments or people would not pay for valuable services and products. I'll bet you pay for many valuable services without having to be threatened first. Such bureaucratic jargon is used to perpetuate a coercive protection racket ran by individuals who refuse to, or are incapable of interacting with others on a mutually voluntary basis. It also demonstrates a lack of understanding of economics and human relations. There are many successful and profitable businesses offering services and products on a purely voluntary basis. They are still profitable even if a percentage of their customers do not pay. It is a part of business; *get over it.* Just because a few people may not pay is no reason the service should be provided at gunpoint.

And if the argument not everyone will pay for services is a reason to not have a voluntary society, then it's an argument against having the involuntary one we have now. Even the IRS admits there are allegedly millions of people who do not pay income taxes.

Some may argue there would be additional "chaos" if there were no compulsory political "laws." This myth is laughable and really needs no explanation. Do you have any idea how many *millions* of political "laws" there are? Neither do I, and I really don't care. But let's use California as an example. If you live in Los Angeles you have the Los Angeles "city" code, the "state" code and the "federal" code you are allegedly required to know and comply with. Each is accompanied by a set of regulations. *Have you ever read all of that*? Then consider the millions of court opinions interpreting and re-interpreting all those "laws." If that were not enough, politicians are constantly making new "laws" and new interpretations *every day*. No one could keep up with that.

The point is that no one knows, or could know the "law." If there is chaos, then it's in the courtrooms when someone is seeking the truth. As I've shown, if I am accused of violating one "statute" a lawyer pretending to be a judge has to "break" at least *eight* of his own sacred "laws" to put me on trial. And don't forget, "judges" can "suspend" their rules any time they want.

Protecting life, liberty and property is a *service* as any other. Regardless of statist theology to the contrary, there's nothing special about this particular service; *it's provided by men and women just like other services are provided.*

What makes this all the more worse is the plain truth that politicians do not acknowledge any obligation to protect anyone anyway. There are many opinions to prove this, the following is just one:

> "The constitution is a charter of negative liberties; it tells the state to let the people alone; ***it does not require the federal government or the states to provide services,*** even so elementary a ***service*** as maintaining law and order." *Bowers v. Devito*, 686 F.2d 616 (emphasis mine).

There you have it, politicians, bureaucrats or whatever you want to call them, openly admitting they have no duty to protect any one. Big surprise there. Re-read the last part again about "maintaining law and order" being a "service."

I'll place the following "laws" together to see which politicians are *lying*:

"Governments derive their just powers from the consent of the governed, and are ***established to protect and maintain individual rights***." Arizona constitution, article II § 2 (emphasis mine).	"The constitution is a charter of negative liberties; it tells the state to let the people alone; ***it does not require the federal government or the states to provide services, even so elementary a service as maintaining law and order***." *Bowers v. Devito*, 686 F.2d 616 (emphasis mine).

If the "constitution" does not require the "state" to provide "law and order", then it doesn't require them to do anything, including administering justice. Get it? There is no clearer evidence of this scam.

THERE IS NO STATE

The fact there is no duty to protect anyone and their property is only one of the ways to prove there is no "state" or "nation." The whole scam is exposed on this issue.

We know pretended "states" are not geographic, they are man-made and consist of so-called "citizens." However, what exactly is a "citizen", "Citizen" or even "Citizen"?

The pretended "Supreme Court" has written:

> "Citizenship is membership in a political society, and implies a duty of allegiance on the part of the member and a duty of protection on the part of the society. These are reciprocal obligations, one being a compensation for the other." *Luria v. U.S.*, 231 U.S. 9, 22.

Notice there must be "reciprocal obligations". Because there is no duty to protect anyone and their property, there is no duty of allegiance. Without these "reciprocal obligations," there are no "citizens" or "Citizens." Because there are no "citizens" there is no "body politic." Without a "body politic" there is no "state" and without "states" there is no "United States" or pretended "nation." Look at it this way:

No duty to protect = no duty of allegiance
no duties = no "citizens"
no "citizens" = no "body politic"
no "body politic" = no "state"
no "state" = no "United States"

No political spin can be put on this. Don't buy into their lies anymore. Do not divert your attention away from the facts and what is happening i.e., your life and property are being controlled without your freely given consent.

The whole scam falls apart on the lack of a duty to protect. It isn't a so-called "conspiracy theory", it's the way it is. That is why lawyers pretending to represent the "state" cannot prove they represent anyone.

I had one radio show host ask me if I thought the "founding fathers" at least had "good intentions". I mentioned that is subjective and irrelevant. The only issue relevant is: **were their services provided on a voluntary basis**? No; so they were the same as we have today, a group of people providing services on a violent/compulsory basis under the guise of consent.

And it doesn't matter if professional, anti-social parasites claim there is a duty to protect because there is only one way a duty to protect can be created. It's only possible if the protection is offered on a voluntary basis like other services. And no, voluntary doesn't mean pay or get shot as it does now.

Just imagine if men and women pretending to be "states" put their guns down and offered their services on a voluntary basis. That would open the door to things bureaucrats fear the most i.e., **competition, choice, freedom and liberty**. Bureaucrats abhor the idea of people controlling their own lives and property and making free choices. Bureaucrats live by a pecking order and can't stand the thought of not being able to control other people. They resent the idea of competition because they would have to provide the service they promise or not get paid. They would have to treat people as, heaven forbid, **equals**. My gosh, bureaucrats would actually be accountable.

Why people accept the PR scam of "politics" and "nations" to this day is a testament to how effective the PR or mind-control is. Let me use one more analogy demonstrating how politicians do business.

You go to Wally's Furniture Store to buy a couch. You

find the one you want; it's $500 and includes delivery to your home. You pay the $500 and go home expecting the couch to be delivered that afternoon as promised by Wally. The afternoon comes and goes, but no couch.

You go back to Wally's the next day and ask why the couch was not delivered. Wally sneers, "What couch?" You tell him you paid $500 for a couch and he told you it would be delivered that afternoon.

Wally arrogantly informs you payment in no way obligated him to give you the couch. You show him the receipt and he again says, *though much louder this time,* "Payment in no way obligated me to give you a couch!" Then, despite your evidence of payment i.e., the receipt, Wally snarls that he's got the "authority" to "treat a particular event that actually happened as not having happened".

That is how men and women pretending to be a "state" operate. And let's not forget you'd also be forced to *continue* paying for a couch you will never receive or get shot. Bureaucrats demand you pay them every year for "protection" they have no duty to provide or they'll kill you. Call me crazy, but I'd rather deal with Wally.

The very idea of competition to protect life, liberty and property is enough to show how ridiculous the concept of a "nation" really is. If you shop at Wally's Furniture you're a customer, not a "citizen." There could be *hundreds* of choices available to choose from; you'd have none of this political crap: "If you don't like it why don't you just leave!" Would each service and its customers be it's own separate "nation"? Sounds silly to me.

To answer the question posed on the back of this book, Yes, it is possible that what we thought was real is nothing more than an elaborate public relations scheme. There is no "state" or "nation". There are no "citizens", Citizens" or "C̲itizens". It's all a scam.

The public relations diverts our attention away from the

fact we are being controlled without our freely given consent; it's called slavery. And that is the problem; being controlled without our freely given consent. That is not freedom; freedom is total control over your life and property. Lysander Spooner demonstrates how insane the concept of government is:

"It cannot be said that men put all their rights into the hands of the government, in order to have them protected; because there can be no such thing as a man's being protected in his rights, any longer than he is allowed to retain them in his own possession. The only possible way, in which any man can be protected in his rights, is to protect him in his own actual possession and exercise of them. And yet our government is absurd enough to assume that a man can be protected in his rights, after he has surrendered them altogether into other hands than his own.

"A man wants his rights protected, solely that he himself may possess and use them, and have the full benefit of them. But if he is compelled to give them up to somebody else, --- to a government, so-called, or to any body else, --- he ceases to have any rights of his own to be protected." *Letter to Grover Cleveland.*

Notwithstanding the lies *inherent* in all politics (politics is a collection of lies), the protection of life, liberty and property is a *service.* There is no reason why this particular service should be set apart from others and provided at the barrel of a machine gun. What a "business" concept; no sales, no accountability, and *everyone* is a paying customer whether they want the service or not. Wally would love it.

And why aren't these services provided on a mutual voluntary basis? Quite simply: **the loss of dominance and control over the people**.

Can you picture a world without Legal Land?